Limited ed

RARE INTEGRITY

LEONIDAS WARREN AND SUSAN BLEDSOE PAYNE, JR.
AUSTIN, CIRCA 1914

HANSEN ALEXANDER

RARE INTEGRITY

A Portrait of L.W. Payne, Jr.

WIND RIVER PRESS

Contents

An Introductory Note

RARE INTEGRITY, A Portrait of L. W. Payne, Jr., directs itself to academics with an interest in Texana, and includes critical articles by Dr. Payne about such national literary figures as Robert Frost, Edwin Arlington Robinson, and E. E. Cummings. The work incorporates important letters to Dr. Payne from J. Frank Dobie at a critical time in young Dobie's career. The work, though, paints a portrait of Professor Payne who acted as an interpreter for these original voices during an era of innovative writing.

All articles and letters in this volume were either edited or abridged for purposes of clarity and space. Recognizing that English is a fluid language, constantly changing, the author has retained spellings the way Dr. Payne wrote them in his writings. For example, the word folklore was often spelled folk-lore in Dr. Payne's time.

Professor Payne's daughter, Mrs. *Sarah Payne Foxworth*, provided the great force behind this biography. She made available boxloads of materials on Dr. Payne's life, traveled several trips to Austin to discuss the book with me and the publisher, and gave financial assistance for research; and when my typewriter broke down, she bought me a new one. She took the lead in seeing the book through to publication, including the details in publishing. She corrected errors in the manuscript and added many insights into Dr. Payne.

Decherd Turner, the distinguished director of the Harry Ransom Humanities Research Center of The University of Texas, read the manuscript and pointed the right direction for publication.

Sarah Beach deciphered the tiny and nearly illegible letters of Edwin Arlington Robinson to Dr. Payne.

Sanford Greenberg, former professor of political science at Kalamazoo College, Kalamazoo, Michigan, read the early chapters of the book and made valuable suggestions.

Through more than two years of research the staff of the Humanities Research Center was extremely helpful. *John Chalmers*, head librarian, provided important help with the Robert Frost material. *John O. Kirkpatrick*, head of cataloging, often stopped in the middle of his own work to help me. *Ellen Dunlop*, research librarian, and her successor, *Cathy Henderson*, tirelessly helped in locating literary estates. I am particularly thankful to my Humanities Research Center friends who worked so hard to get me the material for this book: *Kenny Craven*, *Pat Fox* and *Randy Conner*.

I owe a tremendous debt to my wife, *Judith Endres*, whose love and patience kept me going during the five years of weekends and evenings that it took to write this book.

In addition, I am indebted to the following persons, estates, publishers, agencies, and libraries for permission to print or reprint materials which appear in this book.

Dartmouth College Library for Dr. Payne's letters to Robert Frost.

Permission of *Yale University* for Eugene O'Neill's January 25, 1921 letter to Payne.

George J. Firmage for four E. E. Cummings letters to Payne. Copyright 1986 Cummings Trust.

Alfred A. Knopf, Inc. for a March 31, 1928 letter from Wallace Stevens to Dr. Payne.

A. P. Watt Ltd. to print large extracts from a July 5, 1922 letter from W. B. Yeats to Payne.

Texas State Teachers Association to reprint from *Texas Outlook* magazine "New Viewpoints in History of American Life" and "Scholarship and the Creative Writer."

Mr. Thomas H. Law, Fort Worth, Texas, to quote from his father's article, "Leonidas Warren Payne, Jr. 1873–1945," which appeared in *Studies in English*, 1945–46.

Texas Student Publications to reprint "E. E. Cummings, Painter and Poet," from *The Longhorn Magazine*, December, 1925.

Dallas Morning News to reprint the following book reviews written by Dr. Payne: "Matthias at the Door," portions of "Nicodemus," and "New Book on Thomas Huxley by Professor Clarence Ayres."

Lucille Enix, my editor in Dallas, Texas, to whom I shall be forever grateful for shepherding me through my first book.

The following persons generously shared their memories of Professor Payne: Joseph M. Ray, Alice Cooke, Jack Gray, Mrs. Jack Gray, Mrs. Wilson Hudson, Madge Keeton, Mrs. Thomas F. Hughes, Mrs. John B. Stigall, Allen Ludden, Frank W. Wozencraft, Joe B. Franz, Margaret Cousins, Mrs. Hallie Barton, Mrs. Marietta Payne, Maud Anderson, Judge A. R. Stout, John A. Focht, Oliver H. Radkey, Art Cory, Willis Pratt, Joe Jones, Ellen Brodnax, R. E. Hardaway, Jr., D. M. McKeithan, M. P. S. Spearman, Mrs. Louis Southerland, Mrs. George Marsh, Mary Campbell, Hope Yager, and Nettie Lee Benson.

H.A.

New York, December, 1985

CHAPTER ONE

Rare Integrity

MARIETTA McGregor was more nervous than the other students on a brutally hot morning on the first day of summer school at The University of Texas. Like the other students, Marietta was aware of the fame of the professor they anxiously awaited. But unlike the other students awaiting the entrance of L. W. Payne, Jr., the legendary professor of American literature, Marietta was the girlfriend of Payne's youngest son, John.

The students sat stiffly, almost frozen in their seats. Who wished to look stupid in the presence of a man who entertained Robert Frost, Edgar Lee Masters, and Carl Sandburg in his home? Who wished to do poorly for a professor who was praised by H. L. Mencken, sought out by Ezra Pound? Was not Payne the man who had encouraged and helped the great poet John Crowe Ransom when Ransom was a young professor at Texas?

Just last week, Dr. Payne had shown Marietta a letter from Eugene O'Neill. Marietta could recite the entire letter by heart.

> Provincetown, Mass.
> Jan. 25, 1921
>
> My dear Payne:
>
> I found your letter waiting here when I returned from New York today. Under separate cover, an autographed copy of "Beyond the Horizon" is being mailed to you. It's impossible to get a first edition, however. The book is now starting as a third, and I have no copy of the first but the one in my own library. The one being sent is of the second vintage.
>
> Thank you for the information about "tote." Up here it's rarely used except as a word of comic exaggeration. That was what I meant when Andy uses it.

And thank you for your kind appreciation of the play. Letters like yours make fine reading for an author.

With all best regards,
Sincerely,
EUGENE O'NEILL

Although Marietta appreciated O'Neill, the playwright's Connecticut Yankee bloodline did not absorb her as did the distinguished old family with whom she was involved. Paynes had fought in the Revolutionary War and Civil War. The family traced its lineage back to early eighteenth century Virginia. One Payne, who could say exactly how the bloodlines crossed and meandered back there in the Virginia Tidewater, was Dorothy Payne, better known as Dolly, second wife of James Madison.

Marietta's daydreaming was broken by the entrance of the famous Professor Payne. His tall, lanky frame was dressed in a creme colored suit and he wore a Panama hat.

Payne smiled over the frames of his black-ribboned pince-nez glasses at the thirty-five students. He took off his hat and put down the books he was carrying. Then he turned and faced the class and the students got their first good view of the deep blue eyes and sandy hair of Leonidas Warren Payne, Jr.

"Class," he began, "why is an onion like a grand piano?"

The class was baffled.

He looked once to the left of the class, once to the right of the class, and then looked straight ahead and with a wry grin said, "Because it's smellodious!"

The class laughed and immediately relaxed.

While Dr. Payne launched excitedly into his lecture, Marietta had plenty of time to follow the lecture *and* think about what made Payne such a special teacher. After all, Marietta possessed one of those quick minds which could flash back and forth like lightning, first listening to Payne's words, then musing about Payne's greatness. It was a skill she would employ in later years when she became the first woman assistant attorney general for the State of Texas.

What set Payne apart from many of his colleagues, Marietta

2

could see during that first lecture, lay in his fervor and his attitude toward teaching. Years later Alice Cooke, a colleague of Professor Payne's on the Texas faculty, said, "I believed, like Payne, that you were a teacher first and a scholar second." University of Texas English Professor Robert A. Law affirmed this when he said, ". . . colleagues and students will join in testifying that his conscience was entirely too strong ever to permit neglect of classes in order to write books or articles. His 'teaching load' was always heavy."[1]

Professor Law said, "The secret of his success as a teacher and a scholar lay largely in his own genuine enthusiasm for every task in which he labored."[2] As an undergraduate, University of Texas History Professor Joe B. Franz took Payne's course "Recent American and English Literature."

"What particularly intrigued me," said Franz, "was the way he was able to show his own enthusiasms and dislikes without ever detracting from the authors involved. I often wish that some of these professors who drain the life out of good prose and poetry by being so deathly critical could have watched him in action. His enthusiasm was infectious, and with me it has proved enduring."

"Professor Payne's teaching concern was to inspire the student, to help the student find his own ability, not mold the student in his own image," said Payne's daughter, Sarah Payne Foxworth.

Dr. Payne himself said, "I believe in teaching literature itself rather than too much about it."

He once joked about his philosophy for teaching poetry. "You know my philosophy of balance. Not all good, not all bad. Things are about fifty-fifty. Trouble in this life is bound to come, so you will need a little philosophy. Poetry will give you a fine philosophy, and I'm going to teach you poetry if I have to ram it down your throats."

Like a shepherd, Payne concerned himself as much with his poorer students as he did with his better students. D. M. McKeithan, a colleague, said, "Payne spoke harshly of professors who were only interested in "A" students. Payne said it was *your duty* to help all students. He was very adamant about that."

"Like Sidney Lanier," Professor Payne would say, "I claim to be a preacher of the gospel according to poetry."

3

There was something of the preacher in Dr. Payne. His father-in-law was a Baptist preacher. Payne himself was a founding deacon and Sunday school teacher at University Baptist Church in Austin.

Professor Payne certainly possessed the patience and understanding of a preacher. Marietta had heard stories of Payne's rocky relationship with Edgar Lee Masters, back in the 1920s. Marietta had only been in grade school then, but since she began visiting the Paynes' home, she had heard about Masters' temper and about Mrs. Payne's dislike of Masters.

The tensions began, Marietta learned, back in 1919, when Payne sent Masters a copy of Payne's anthology, *History of American Literature*. It was Payne's practice to send manuscripts or copies of his anthologies to authors for comments.

In *History of American Literature*, Dr. Payne had said Masters discovered free verse after reading poems in *Poetry* magazine edited by Harriet Monroe. There in the pages of *Poetry*, Dr. Payne wrote, Masters "recognized at once that it was exactly the medium which he needed." And Dr. Payne called *Spoon River Anthology*, which had vaulted Masters onto the national literary stage in 1915, "frank even to vulgarity and brutality."

Masters sent an angry reply, earning ever after the dislike of Mrs. Payne. Masters did not comment on *Spoon River*. He was irritated enough about the issue of *Poetry's* influence. Masters said he did not know where Dr. Payne got the idea about *Poetry's* influence, but Masters said it certainly did not come from him.[3]

Despite Masters' testy letter, Professor Payne bore him no grudge. And a week later, having calmed down, Masters wrote Payne a friendly letter telling Payne he wished Payne were in Chicago to help him proof a new book of poems, probably *Starved Rock*.[4]

In Professor Payne's quest to understand the creative process, a quest that propelled his tireless proofreading and study of the authors he examined and taught, he kept calm, because he understood that Masters and other writers had a necessity to vent their emotions. Like a parent, Payne knew he had to wait for the emotional crisis of the writer to pass. And Payne knew that Masters

4

was an overworked man who toiled as a lawyer while writing poetry.

Keeping one's calm took patience and understanding, and L. W. Payne, Jr. was endowed with an abundance of both.

Who else but Dr. Payne could scribble on an envelope this notation after receiving a tough letter from Masters? "Masters was severe on me—but severer on himself."

Yet Dr. Payne was more than patient and understanding. Joseph M. Ray, President of The University of Texas, El Paso, from 1960–1968, worked for seven years as a typist for Payne while working his way through school. When Dr. Payne became president of the University Faculty Club, he gave Ray an additional job as night boy there. "He peeped into the kitchen once," Ray said,"and saw me eating my meal at a small table; the very next meal I was seated at the table with faculty members, and ate that way the rest of my time there."

But terms like "patient, understanding, nice guy," are insufficient to describe L. W. Payne, Jr. Lon Tinkle, the biographer of J. Frank Dobie, the writer Payne probably helped the most, put it best when he said Payne was a man of "rare integrity, even of nobility."[5]

Upon the occasion of Dr. Payne's death in 1945, Stark Young, the versatile southern writer, quoted Christ's words to describe how Payne gave of himself to others: "I come that ye might have life and have it more abundantly."[6]

Two men of immense patience helped Stark Young during his long career. One, Maxwell Perkins, served as editor of Young's books published by Scribner's. The other, Professor Payne, encouraged Young's first work, proofread those early manuscripts, reviewed all his books as they appeared, acted as his bibliographer, and collected first editions of his works.[7]

Joining the Texas faculty in 1907 after taking his M.A. in English from Columbia University, Stark Young taught drama while penning a flood of poetry and plays in his spare time. In 1909, Young created a vehicle for his plays, the famous Curtain Club. Professor and Mrs. Payne were among its most supportive patrons. In fact, the Paynes were supportive of all of Young's artistic endeavors, which included novels, translations, criticism, and painting. Young once said that the Paynes had shown more interest in his poetry than anybody else in Texas,[8] which was probably an understatement. Dr. Payne even helped to publicize Young. In 1934 Dr. Payne sent six hundred notices to small newspapers and teachers' groups about *So Red the Rose*, Young's bestselling novel which charted the destruction of the Old South by the Civil War.[9]

Since we like those who praise us, it is understandable that Young became very attached to the Payne family. When Stark went on a holiday to Italy in 1909, he bought Mrs. Payne a cameo necklace at Dr. Payne's request. In March 1909, Young wrote the following poem to Mrs. Payne. The poem was to have been published by *Scribner's Magazine* in 1910, but it did not appear in print.

"Song for a Child"

Hast thou not seen the quiet blue
That bends from out the quiet skies,
And watcheth thee the long day through?
It is thy mother's eyes.

Hast thou seen the tender sun
That lights thy heaven thereabove,
And sends the stars when day is done?
It is thy mother's love.

Hast thou heard each leaf and tree
Forget the daytime's heat and noise,
While sleep comes stealing over thee?
It is thy mother's voice.

The Paynes' third child, Sarah Farnham Payne, was born in January, 1910. Stark doted on Sarah the rest of his life. Today, his poem, which is signed by him at the bottom, rests on Sarah's living room wall in Dallas.

The last legacy Young left to Texas as he departed for Amherst College in 1915, was the founding of *The Texas Review*, which became the *Southwest Review* in 1924.

Young quit Amherst in 1921 and moved to New York City, where he spent most of the rest of his life, gaining fame for his translations of Chekhov, his novel *So Red the Rose*, his books about the theater, and his drama column in *The New Republic*. Young did travel back and forth to Austin, in large part because his sister lived there. On those many occasions he often dropped in to see the man who had helped him in the beginning, L. W. Payne, Jr.

Among the compliments Stark Young gave L. W. Payne, Jr., two are especially worth repeating. Young praised the work of his friends and helped younger writers, just as Payne had helped him. The second compliment Stark gave Dr. Payne appeared in the form of an article he wrote entitled "Obituaries" in *The English Bulletin*, University of Texas, v.56, 1928. P—, of course, is Payne.

"Obituaries"

Obituaries about men still alive may seem strange enough, but about P—, they are more than plausible. You can see P— with that glow and sweetness with which we look back at people down the long avenues of time, and with which saints surround themselves in a heavenly vista.

"Tell me about Cummings," P—was asking almost as soon as we had sat down. "He's the playboy of American poetry, isn't he?"

"Cummings is fine."

"But I'm getting worried about Cummings, he's a bad boy, he's not getting forward—" he goes on talking about "Him" and how much he liked parts of it, but adds, firmly enough, that "Him" was written some time ago, and that he'll have to desert Cummings if he doesn't get a new start, something is the matter with him, he doesn't grow up, and it's time.

He asks about Sherwood Anderson, when shall we have something new from him, and how does "Strange Interlude" seem when it is acted?—and so on and so on, there is a great deal he wants the news of; down here in this country, he says, down South here, we're so far off. I answer as busily as I can, though I am really thinking more of P—himself, whom I have not seen for several years. I look at his tall, thin body, rather worn now at fifty, at the kind, happy, pathetic eyes, the wide, smiling mouth, I hear the friendly, slow voice. Then he is asking about my work, he has all my books, he wants me to do this now or do that, he has been hoping I'd gone on with—. It is all familiar to me coming from him. No wonder my sister, who is with me, keeps saying when we are back in the automobile that she never saw so sweet a face, like a saint's.

I am thinking of P—'s generous interest and concern long ago when I was writing my first lines, of that unending assurance that he wanted me to turn out well, write beautifully, and that art was a natural impulse, not a luxury. There is no need to stay on that— *namque tu solebas meas esse aliquid putare nugas*—one way of saying it is that P— is the sort of man who tempts you to boast, even to brag, of your little achievements, to lie about them almost, just because you know how much pleasure you will give him.

Without intense study and exhaustive reading P—knows about the man he reads the one central truth, which few ever quite know. This great gift of creative generosity and warmth of heart that he has, enables him to see this man as the man himself wishes to be seen; and thus there appears to P— the characteristic soul and flavor of the other. And it is within this character that he wishes him to succeed, not as something that he is not. He wishes for your own kind of perfection, and senses your desire and motion toward it. He becomes your best public because more and more of you goes where more and more of you is welcome; and your best critic because he helps you to judge what you have done, not by the achievement of others, but by what is possible to you.

You must smile to think of what would happen if you tried to tell P— these virtues of his. That grin, that drawl he brought with him from Alabama—

"Oh, shucks, your blarney! I just like to see a man do good stuff, anybody does," and by then his hand would be reaching out for something you ought to blow the horn for, the page is turned down, listen here—

STARK YOUNG

8

CHAPTER TWO

Alabama and the Early Years

*L*EONIDAS Warren Payne, Jr. was born on July 12, 1873, in Auburn, Alabama. He was named after his father, a Civil War veteran, who made tin ware, farmed a little, made loans to neighbors, and even served as postmaster of Auburn.

Despite the death of his mother, Mary Jane Payne, in 1878, a happy, bookish atmosphere permeated the boyhood home of the future professor. His father and older sister Fannie read him Shakespeare from his earliest years. By the age of ten or eleven, the industrious lad had read all the comedies and tragedies and most of the histories in the family's bulky illustrated volume of Shakespeare.

Payne's first job as a boy was to check brick and lumber as it was hauled in to build his future alma mater, Alabama Polytechnic Institute. Young Payne calculated the number of bricks on a wagon by counting the number in rows in depth and the number in length, and then by multiplying them together.

After attending Alecia Milton's private elementary school and the local public high school, Payne entered Alabama Polytechnic Institute (now Auburn University) in 1888. At Auburn there was no subject he did not master. He ranked as the best student in English and stood first in his class in mathematics. In addition, he excelled in botany, chemistry, physics, history, and agriculture. He read French and Latin with ease and German with some fluency. His fellow students elected him class orator in 1892 for a speech about George Washington. It was understandable that when the Alabama Polytechnic class of 1892 assembled for graduation at 10 a.m. on June 15, its valedictorian in the literary course was Leonidas Warren Payne, Lee County, Alabama.

Upon graduating Payne was awarded a fellowship at Alabama

Polytechnic to pursue a Masters in English. In addition, he served as assistant librarian and assistant to the president of the college. During his two years as assistant librarian, he practically managed the library, and developed a catalogue of the library that remained in use at the time of his departure in 1895. Payne also taught for the first time during this period when he filled in for an ailing history professor.

His scholarship and industry made a good impression on his Alabama Polytechnic professors in both undergraduate and graduate school. C. C. Thach, one of his English professors and later president of Alabama Polytechnic, said Payne possessed an unusual taste and discrimination for literature, one that could not always be acquired.

Equipped with his literary instincts and an M.S. in English, Payne elected in 1895 to teach English and Modern Languages in the Southwest Alabama Agricultural School, Evergreen, Alabama.

During those first years after Auburn, Payne worked to broaden his understanding of the human condition and its relationship to literature. He began to develop a more progressive outlook, an outlook that would allow him to be one of the first to understand, if not embrace, the literary rebellion of the approaching twentieth century. Although Payne's grandfather had owned slaves for a time, Payne had supported "Negro" voting in an undergraduate debate, arguing that literacy should not be a criterion for voting. He suggested that "Negroes" who could not read or write be allowed to vote because, Payne said, many Americans who were illiterate had made great sacrifices for America. The history of our present century shows how far ahead of his time he was. Politicians still hotly debated literacy as a voting criterion in the 1960s, seventy years after Payne's arguments at Auburn. Above all, Payne was developing a classic liberal attitude, not the liberalism of nineteenth century free trade or twentieth century liberalism of progressive politics, but rather the ancient definition of openmindedness.

In the manner of Thomas Jefferson, Payne began taking notes on his reading and logged them in a bound journal in late 1894. In his journal for December 6, 1894, Payne wrote that he read "The Merchant of Venice" to an audience of three undergraduates preparing for an exam on the play. Payne reported that one boy fell asleep during the reading and snored.

In his journal for December 21, 1894, Payne noted that he had been reading Oliver Goldsmith, specifically *Traveller, Deserted Village, Vicar of Wakefield,* and *Heavenly Twins.* Payne admired the position assumed by the "new woman" as she appeared in *Heavenly Twins.*

Payne wrote at some length in his journal attacking the double standard for men and women, "The idea that men should be as virtuous and as uncontaminated as the women to whom they attach themselves is nothing but just and right.

"The very vilest of men are never satisfied with anything but the very purest of women. There is much injustice in this, for if a man is so weak as to allow his passions to sway him, and he commits such excesses as will tend to tear down his physical health and moral constitution, he is unworthy the confidence and purity of an innocent maiden who knows not sin. I believe in woman's rights so far as they effect the virtuous and marital relations of man and wife. It is a step toward a higher plane when the purer sex revolts against the iniquities of the sterner sex. God be with them in their efforts, for they have a mountain to move."

Payne's interest in virtuousness in his journal may have been influenced by a matter very close to his heart in February, 1895. He was then worried about religious differences between himself and Mary Susan Bledsoe, daughter of a Baptist minister. Payne was a Methodist. Obviously thinking of marrying Miss Bledsoe, Payne declared in his journal that he had too high an opinion of the intelligence of Miss Bledsoe's father to think he would contend against his daughter's happiness simply on the ground of denominational differences.

Payne in fact had taken the teaching job at Southwest Alabama Agricultural School in Evergreen, Alabama because it was relatively near La Fayette, Alabama, where Sue Bledsoe lived.

They had met at a teacher's institute in 1892, when Sue was only sixteen. Payne immediately fell in love with her and courted her for five years. Her father forbade her writing him from January, 1894 to January, 1895 because she was, he said, too young. Payne, nevertheless, had proposed marriage in December, 1893, as the following letter reveals. Miss Bledsoe referred to Payne as "Tim," her pet name for him.

> Auburn, Ala
> Dec. 6, 1893
>
> My darling "Sue":—
>
> The fact that I love you more and more and that I will never consider that I have reached the crowning point of my life until I can call you *my own* in very truth, becomes more and more evident every day of my life . . .
>
> I have no fortune to lay at your feet; I have no title—or vainglorious pedigree to crown you withal; but I have a heart, and let us hope it is a heart of gold, and that it is yours completely . . .
>
> You have told me that you loved me, and that you would prefer no other! You have admitted that you were my sweetheart and I yours; but I must yet ask you for more. Will you, my darling girl, promise me that one day, God willing, I may press you to my heart and call you wife? . . .
>
> Answer me at once and set me at ease . . .
>
> *Yours*
> "TIM"

From January, 1895 until their wedding in October, 1897, they corresponded, and Payne visited his future bride several times in La Fayette.

When Payne set out to travel to La Fayette in October, 1897, a yellow fever epidemic plagued Alabama. Men carrying shotguns guarded the entrances to villages as part of the statewide quarantine which included detention camps. Friends told Payne, "Of course you will postpone your wedding day, you can't possibly get there." Payne got there.

Instead of trying to run the blockade through Montgomery, Payne made a three-day perilous trip of 160 miles over land and by railroad in a circular route from Evergreen to La Fayette.

Payne traveled by buggy to Searight, Alabama. He wanted to spend the night there but the mayor kicked him out of town. So he spent the night in a cotton seed fertilizer plant, where he tried to keep warm by covering himself with cotton seed. The next day Payne boarded a train to Columbus, Georgia and spent most of the ride answering questions from quarantine officers.

Payne had planned to stay in Columbus overnight. But the uncertainty of the quarantine compelled him to continue on to La Fayette the same day. "A few more quarantine officers," wrote Payne, "and a few more hours of riding and I jumped off in La Fayette and hastened to my loved one."

Leonidas Warren Payne, Jr. and Mary Susan Bledsoe were married at 6:45 a.m., Wednesday, October 27, 1897.

Payne taught in Evergreen until 1899 when he accepted a position in the State Normal School, Jacksonville, Alabama. C. Dauqette, the school's president, saw Payne teach for one year and said, "He can get more work out of students than any other teacher with whom I was ever associated." Dauqette added, "I believe that if you were to search the south you could not find a man who will give you more genuine service and satisfaction than Mr. Payne."

Jacksonville reelected Payne and raised his salary for the second year, but he turned the offer down.

The ambitious teacher applied to the doctoral programs in English at The University of Pennsylvania and Harvard and to the Political Science program at Columbia. The University of Pennsylvania offered Payne a fellowship and he accepted it.

Mrs. Payne decided to remain in La Fayette and teach school that fall of 1899 when Payne went to Philadelphia to begin doctoral work. On December 10, Sue gave birth to their first child, Bledsoe.

As a graduate student at The University of Pennsylvania, colleagues remembered Payne as one of the most sincere and devoted students the graduate faculty ever knew, said Clarence G. Child, one of his professors.

Payne's career as a critic began while studying at Penn. His earliest published article appeared in 1900 in the *Sewanee Review*. That first article examined the stories of James Lane Allen. Payne's other *Sewanee Review* articles published during his graduate school

13

days discussed Thackeray, Sidney Lanier, and the Elizabethan poet Humphrey Gifford.

L. W. Payne, Jr. was awarded the Ph.D. in 1904. His graduation from Penn brought a change of positions from academia to the publishing world. He landed a job at the J. P. Lippincott Company as an editor revising *Worcester's Dictionary*. Mrs. Payne left La Fayette the next year, 1905, to join him in Philadelphia. Their second child, Warren, was born there in February, 1906. In March, 1906, the Paynes left Philadelphia when Dr. Payne chose to teach English at Louisiana State University.

Permanently elected assistant professor of English at LSU in June, 1906, Dr. Payne turned down the offer. He did not like the scenery around LSU's Baton Rouge campus, especially the flat lands of the Mississippi. When Dr. Morgan Callaway, head of the English department at The University of Texas, invited Payne to teach at Texas, he accepted the offer. In doing so, Payne resigned from the LSU faculty to accept a Texas offer of lower academic rank, instructor, and less certain prospects for advancement. "But I have never regretted it," he told his good friend and University of Texas colleague, Robert Law, many years later.

CHAPTER THREE

A Folklore Father

WHILE on the editorial staff of J. B. Lippincott in Philadelphia, Payne had started what became *A Word-List from East Alabama*, published in *Dialect Notes*, III, 1908–1909, and in the *Alabama Historical Quarterly*. *A Word-List* contained 3,000 entries of colloquial words and phrases in common use among all classes in East Alabama.

The American Dialect Society, whose purpose was to publish an American Dialect Dictionary on a scale of the great English Dialect Dictionary, published *Dialect Notes*. Payne belonged to this Dialect Society. He had wanted to include an account of the East-Alabama dialect in the Oxford Dictionary but the editors had turned him down.

Payne's *Word-List* drew surprising interest in Texas and convinced him that a folklore society could exist in Texas. He did not have to wait long.

John A. Lomax, a Mississippi native, had studied at Texas under Professor Callaway as an undergraduate and Callaway had told Lomax to forget cowboy songs and turn to Beowulf.[1] Nevertheless when Lomax prepared to leave Harvard in 1907 to teach at Texas A&M after a year of collecting songs and ballads of the cowboy, his Harvard mentor, Professor G. L. Kittredge, urged him to organize a Texas Folklore Society.

Lomax had met Payne during Lomax's senior year at The University of Texas. Now the two old acquaintances agreed to meet in Austin to discuss the possibility of a Folklore Society. The accounts of where the discussion took place differ. Lomax said they met in Payne's study on Pearl Street. Payne's version, offered during the twenty-fifth anniversary dinner of The Texas Folklore Society in 1934, put the critical talk at sunset on The University of

Texas campus. The Texas Folklore Society reprinted Dr. Payne's discussion of this important event.

"I Was Here When the Woods Were Burnt"
by L. W. Payne, Jr.

"It was written in the stars centuries before I was born that I was to become a bred-in-the-bones Texan; if not by nativity, then surely by adoption. If I had been born at the beginning of the nineteenth century instead of near the beginning of its fourth quarter, I would in all probability have been one of the earliest Anglo-Saxon pioneers in Texas. Perhaps I might have heard and answered the call of Moses Austin; or if not that, surely I would have been attracted to Texas by the suave blandishments or the sane statesmanship of Stephen F. Austin. In my youth in Alabama I often saw whole families moving to Texas, and I sometime heard also a great deal about other individuals fleeing to Texas. Whenever a person got into trouble over in Alabama, involved in a murder or a stealing or a shot-gun wedding, he suddenly disappeared; and when people asked where he could be, the invariable answer was: "Gone to Texas." So you see it was inevitable that eventually I would have to come to Texas. I refuse, however, to divulge which one of the above mentioned reasons made it possible for my neighbors in Alabama to wag their heads when I disappeared from my native state and, in answer to the familiar query as to my whereabout, reply in a doleful tone: "Gone to Texas."

If I was not in Texas "when the first woods were burnt," I got here at least before all the woods were burnt. I recall my first experience at one of these "woods burnings." I stood by and watched the mule-eared jack rabbits, the furtive coyotes, the bristling wolves, the wambling armadillos, the swift deer, the lumbering buffaloes, and the arrow-like piasanos hastening away from the approaching flames and vanishing over the hills toward the setting sun. I said to myself: "Surely Texas is the happy hunting ground, not only for game but for folklore of all kinds as well," and I was content to set up my *lares* and *penates* on the edge of the burnt woods.

It so happened that when I came to Texas I was much interested in the subject of folk speech or dialect, for I was just at that time completing a monograph on the dialect of East Alabama. It was in the fall of 1906 that I came to Texas at the invitation of my friend

16

Dr. Morgan Callaway, Jr., and by the spring of 1908 I had sent the manuscript of my monograph, *A Word-List from East Alabama*, to the secretary of the American Dialect Society for publication. At some time between 1906 and 1908 I had met a young Associate Professor of English from the Texas A&M College named John Avery Lomax. He too was interested in the lore of the folk, and on the basis of our mutual interest in folk materials we soon became warm friends. His particular interest at that time—an interest by the way which he has maintained, somewhat intermittently to be sure, up to the present moment as is evidenced by the announcement of his book *American Ballads and Folk Songs* for April publication by the Macmillan Company—was cowboy songs and ballads. I think it was during the session of 1909–1910 that Mr. Lomax accepted a Sheldon Fellowship from Harvard University for the special purpose of collecting the songs and ballads of the cowboy, for I remember that I was enabled to add one or two songs to his collection by calling on my early Texas freshmen English students for themes on cowboy songs that they knew or had heard of. I think, too, it was in the fall of 1908 that we had our first talk about the possibility of collecting Texas folk songs and dialectal peculiarities, but no definite mode of procedure was decided upon at that time. We may also have said something about the possibility of forming a society to aid each of us in working out his special interest.

I recall rather clearly the crucial conversation between Mr. Lomax and myself which led to the decision to bring the Texas Folk-Lore Society into being. It occurred immediately after the Thanksgiving football game between Texas and the A&M College in 1909. The game was played on the old Clark Field down where the new Power House and Engineering Building now stand.

We began to talk about various forms of folklore in Texas, and Mr. Lomax told me something about his experiences in visiting round-ups and cow camps in his search for cowboy songs and lingo. He said that Professor Kittredge of Harvard had suggested to him that it might be a good thing to found a Texas branch of the American Folklore Society in order to facilitate the collection of the native songs and ballads as well as other forms of folklore. Mr. Lomax further said that he didn't see how such a society could be formed unless somebody here at the University would take the initiative, for the University was the only proper place in Texas for such an undertaking to be fostered. I immediately responded that I would undertake to work up an interest in folklore among the members of the University faculty if Mr. Lomax would do the same among the faculty at the A&M College. I recall that by this time we had reached the southwest corner of the campus in our stroll, a spot near where the Education Building or Sutton Hall now stands. Around us were the mesquites and other native trees and shrubs, and as darkness was settling down on that Thanksgiving Day, November 25, 1909, we agreed to propose the formation of a Texas Folk-Lore Society at the coming meeting of the Texas State Teachers Association at Dallas during the Christmas holidays. Seven years later Mr. Lomax, in his paper on *Unexplored Treasures of Texas Folklore* in the first number of the Publications of the Texas Folk-Lore Society (1916), generously gives me the credit of suggesting the organization, saying, "Dr. Payne was not only the first President of the Society, but he was likewise first to suggest the organization; and history, therefore, should thus early recognize him as the founder of the Texas branch of the American Folklore Society." I have never claimed this honor for myself alone, for as I remember the occasion it was a purely collaborative interest that brought forth the idea of forming the Society, and I have always considered myself as one of the two co-founders, and have always accorded my colleague credit on an absolute fifty-fifty basis. In response to his suggestion that Professor Kittredge wanted to see a branch of the American Folklore Society founded in Texas I perhaps said, "Well, let's found one;" but if Mr. Lomax said that we ought to found such a society and I said "Let's found one," which one of us was the first to propose the organization?

The next thing in order was the division of labor in effecting the organization. Since we two were apparently the only persons in the state actively interested in forming the Society, we would naturally be expected to do the preliminary work in launching the movement; and we had a notion, or perhaps I should say a sort of secret ambition, that we might be elected to the two chief offices, the presidency and secretaryship of the Society. I have often jokingly remarked that John nominated me for president and I nominated him for secretary, and each of us was literally *unanimously* elected, for each of us got but a single vote. But the real truth is that we merely laid our plans and our friends did the dirty work for us. Mr. Lomax suggested that I take the job of drawing up the constitution of the proposed society and make some general preliminary statement about the plans and purposes of such a society; and for his job he would begin to shell the woods for members to join us in the undertaking. He had a wide acquaintance in the state, and he proposed to correspond with, solicit support from, and interview various influential individuals in the interest of the undertaking.

I wrote my friend Professor H. M. Belden at the University of Missouri, who had formed a folklore society in his state, and asked him for suggestions. He sent me several leaflets issued by the Missouri Folklore Society, and from these I got some ideas about how to proceed in formulating a plan for the Texas society. I happen to have preserved the original holograph of our plan, and on reading it over during the past week I find that the organization of the Society today is practically identical with that first plan of organization.

As it turned out, neither Mr. Lomax nor I was able to attend the teachers' meeting at Dallas, and so we entrusted our plans to Professor Killis Campbell, who happened to have a paper to read in the English section of the T.S.T.A. that year. It was, then, on December 29, 1909, at the meeting of the English Section of the Texas State Teachers Association at Dallas that Dr. Campbell introduced the resolution to organize the Texas Folk-Lore Society by appointing the two main officers, who were to be entrusted with the working out of the details of the organization.

Pretty soon after this event Mr.Lomax and I had worked up an initial charter membership of sixty-six persons. I had convassed the University faculty and Mr. Lomax had enrolled a number of members from the A&M College and from other sections of the State, and thus a substantial number of charter members were secured. We then decided that the enrollment of charter members should be extended to April 1, 1910, and by that time ninety-two persons were formally enrolled in the Society.

In June, 1910, President Mezes invited Mr. Lomax to come to Austin to become Secretary of the Board of Regents and general publicity agent for the University, and from that date on we were able to confer frequently and to work effectively in the interest of the Folk-Lore Society. In the fall of 1910 we began active preparations for our first annual program. I have cause to remember this fact distinctly, for it fell my lot to provide the program for the first meeting. Naturally I called upon my colleagues in the University faculty to prepare most of the papers. We met in the old Faculty Room, No. 48, in the old Main Building, over there in the northeast corner of the first floor of the east wing, on April 8, 1911. I have preserved both the preliminary holograph and the final typed copy of that program. We had two sessions, one in the afternoon and another in the evening. I led off in the afternoon session with the President's Address, "Preliminary Survey of Folklore Interests in Texas." Then came Dr. R. H. Griffith with "Method of Study in Folklore," and Dr. R. A. Law with "The Pronunciation of Some Huguenot Proper Names in South Carolina." Dr. Sylvester Primer of the German department spoke on "German Folklore in Texas;" and between these four papers by members of the University faculty were sandwiched three other papers by three good women folklorists, Mrs. Lillie T. Shaver on "Indian Customs," Mrs. Bess Brown Lomax on "The Ballad of the Boll Weevil," and Miss Adina de Zavala of San Antonio on "A Ballad of the Missionary Period." Two other papers were offered by men, one by Mr. Theo G. Lemmons of Dallas on "Some Little Known Myths of the Moqui Pueblos" and another by our former colleague at Texas, Dr. Herbert E. Bolton, who had recently gone to Stanford University in California, on "Religious Beliefs and Customs of the Hasinai Indians," but in the absence of their respective authors, these papers were read by title only. The evening public session was held in the University Auditorium, situated in the old north wing of the Main Building, the occasion being the address of Professor Bliss Perry of Harvard, whom Mr. Lomax had induced to come to Texas as our first distinguished visiting lecturer. In later programs we had two other Harvard celebrities to deliver addresses before the Society, Professors Barrett Wendell and George Lyman Kittredge; and other distinguished visiting lecturers were Seuman McManus, the noted Irish story writer and folklorist and Professor Louise Pound of the University of Nebraska.

The rest of the story is well known. The Society has continued regularly to meet in annual session except for an interregnum of four years from 1918 to 1922, due to America's entrance into the World War and the after effects. It has published, now, eleven annual volumes of folklore papers and has definitely established itself as the very best of all the state folklore societies in the nation.

My own interest in the Society has been intense and continuous, though I must say that recently I have been shifting the major part of the work of the Society to younger shoulders. The secretaries of a society of this kind deserve more credit for its success than do the

Presidents. Those who have served as secretary of our Society successively are John A. Lomax, Professor W. P. Webb, both from Texas, and Dr. Stith Thompson, editor of our first printed volume and now a distinguished English professor and folklorist at the University of Indiana, and Professor J. Frank Dobie of our own faculty who has been the secretary and editor of the Society continuously since 1922. The Founders' celebration on the twenty-fifth anniversary of the birth of the Society ought not to be passed without a vote of thanks to these faithful servants and to all the past presidents and other officers and to those who have contributed papers to the programs and the published volumes, all of whom in their joint efforts have helped materially in making the Texas Folklore Society the success it is today.

Fellow-folklorists and friends, I cannot tell you how deeply I appreciate the signal honor which you have conferred upon me and my colleague by dedicating this dinner on the twenty-fifth anniversary of the Texas Folklore Society to the founders. I am sure that I voice the sentiment of my co-founder when I say this occasion will be ever cherished by us as one of the most felicitous events of our lives."

Professor Payne served as president of the Folklore Society from 1909–1911. During this period the society's first publication appeared, in 1910, as a circular by Payne which listed the officers, explained the kinds of participation, and stated the purposes of the society.[2] The first of the official Publications of the Folk-Lore Society of Texas was printed in 1916. Professor Payne and R. E. Dudley contributed "Texas Play-party Songs and Games."

In 1927, Dr. Payne wrote, "I look upon the formation of this Society as one of my most important contributions to the general educational welfare of Texas."

It was through a mutual love of folklore that Professor Payne established a long friendship with the great poet of the American prairie, Carl Sandburg. Sandburg visited Austin numerous times to do benefits for The Texas Folklore Society. Sandburg, in his earthy manner, took to calling Professor Payne "Old Scout" and "Flummywister."

Sandburg's first visit to Austin and his first meeting with Dr. Payne occurred in the spring of 1923 when he arrived in Texas to lecture and talk folklore. On that occasion Sandburg met two other famous Texas folklorists, John Lomax and J. Frank Dobie.

Dr. Payne next visited with Sandburg in the summer of 1924 in Chicago, where Dr. Payne had gone to meet his editor at Rand McNally. Payne called on Sandburg at the offices of *The Chicago Daily News*, where Sandburg worked, mostly writing movie reviews. Sandburg was sitting in a dark office fingering a big black suitcase full of typewritten sheets, when Payne met him. The sheets were the manuscript of Sandburg's monumental biography of Abraham Lincoln.

As Payne entered the office, he saw Sandburg looking for a certain chapter of which he had no duplicate copy elsewhere, intending to put these particular sheets in his breast pocket for safety while away from the office making his rounds of the movies. Sandburg read to Payne passages of the Lincoln biography. Sandburg told Professor Payne he was writing "a new kind of biography of Lincoln—a real, honest-to-goodness, everyday man—not a formal biography, but a sort of factual novel—a true story which would be really stronger and more fascinating than fiction, a sort of imaginative, creative work based on the actual words of those who knew and loved and wondered at and talked with Abraham Lincoln." That was how Payne first saw Sandburg's book, *Abraham Lincoln, The Prairie Years*.

The book was published in 1926 and Dr. Payne reviewed it favorably for *The Dallas Morning News*. Dr. Payne also wrote Sandburg and urged him to write a sequel. Sandburg did and the result: *Abraham Lincoln: The War Years*, was awarded the Pulitzer Prize for History in 1940.

In late January, 1929, Sandburg came to Austin for another benefit for The Texas Folklore Society; Sandburg gave a song and poetry recital at the Austin High School Auditorium. Sandburg returned to visit Austin and see Dr. Payne in 1935 and 1943. The 1935 visit is well-documented.

Sandburg stayed in the Payne home during his visit and fascinated his hosts by eating the white yoke around his hard-boiled eggs and then eating the yellow.

Marietta McGregor spent a lot of time with Sandburg during his visit and remembered that, "He was a vigorous, stocky, swarthy man with a shock of white hair that fell over his forehead when he talked." Mrs. Payne gave Marietta and John Payne the task of taking Sandburg to a beer garden where he could drink, since Mrs. Payne did not permit drinking in the Payne household. John brought his Sigma Chi fraternity brother, Jack Gray, the Texas basketball star who pioneered the one-handed jump shot, with him also. The three collegians and Sandburg left the Payne residence around 4 p.m. and drove to Pike's Place, near East 7th Street in Austin. Marietta recalled being seated on rough wooden chairs at a wooden table where sawdust had been sprinkled liberally all over the floor.

Jack Gray remembers, "We ate spaghetti, which was all we could afford, and drank beer. We didn't return to the Paynes' until midnight." Gray recalls, "Dr. Payne was worried. He was up smoking."

On Wednesday, March 27, Professors Payne, Walter P. Webb, and Roy Benedict went with Sandburg to Southwestern University to hear Sandburg lecture.

They stopped at the Sam Bass Cafe in Round Rock for beer, excepting Payne, who probably had a soft drink. On the return trip they stopped at a rival cafe where Sam Bass had been shot. They did not reach Austin until 1 a.m., and even then Sandburg was still going strong. He went to Professor Walter Webb's home where he and Webb talked till 3:30.

A notable absence for the journey to Southwestern, his alma mater, was J. Frank Dobie. In truth, Dobie and Sandburg spent a great deal of time together whenever Sandburg came to Austin. They were remarkably similar men, earthy by nature and tireless writers. They were politically progressive and both suffered something for it. The University of Texas eventually let Dobie go for sympathizing with University of Texas president Homer Rainey, who had been fired by the University regents for defending academic freedom. Two years before his 1935 visit, Sandburg had lost the friendship of the politically conservative Robert Frost by supporting Roosevelt and the New Deal.[3]

The day after his Southwestern lecture, Sandburg delivered an evening lecture at Hogg Memorial Auditorium on the University campus. Marietta and John and Jack Gray took Sandburg to the lecture. Sandburg opened his performance by playing a banjo and half sang and half read his poetry. At one point in the performance, Sandburg surprised his three young hosts when he said, "Since I've been in Austin, I've been associated with men of action, John Payne and Jack Gray." The face of the embarrassed Gray turned crimson. But the other students howled with enthusiasm. Sandburg later sent an autographed picture to Gray.

John Payne, Marietta McGregor, J. Frank Dobie, and Jack Gray were not the only ones who entertained Sandburg on his Austin visits. Richard Armour, the author of sixty-two books, lived with the Paynes for a year. Once he took Sandburg around the Austin area. Said Armour, "Of lifetime importance to me was learning from Sandburg several push-up exercises that he said had given him strength and fitness. One exercise, using the arms of the chair, was quite difficult." Armour said he nevertheless mastered the difficult push-up and in later years demonstrated it for Johnny Carson on "The Tonight Show."

Many persons share the great misconception that J. Frank Dobie founded The Texas Folklore Society. The *Western Review* shared this misconception in 1965 when it stated that "without departmental support, but with the approval of George Lyman Kittredge, Stith Thompson, John Lomax, and Leonardus [sic] Payne, Dobie helped to found the Texas Folklore Society in 1915." The Texas Folklore Society was founded in 1909, not 1915, and Dobie did not found or assist in founding the society.

J. Frank Dobie's interest in folklore was, however, longstanding and preceded his arrival in Austin as an instructor at The University of Texas. This fact overshadows Dobie's own protests that he had never heard of the word "folklore" before being invited to join The Texas Folklore Society. Payne and Lomax, nonetheless, provided a vehicle for folklore gathering by the man who became the most famous writer identified with Texas.

CHAPTER FOUR

Fighting for Dobie

*I*T was appropriate that when Stark Young, Payne's first "literary son," left Texas in 1915, Payne prepared to know J. Frank Dobie.

Dobie had arrived on the Texas campus in the fall of 1914 to teach English. Like Stark Young, Dobie had earned his M.A. in English from Columbia University.

Upon the urging of Stith Thompson, the secretary, Dobie apparently joined the Folklore Society in 1914.[1] Dobie was not, however, very involved in the Society in the beginning and did not contribute to the Society's first regular publication in 1916.

Many English faculty members considered Dobie crude because of his earthy, beer-drinking persona and his lack of enthusiasm for getting a Ph.D. Dobie also seemed more interested in cowboys than Hamlet. These aspects of his personality did not endear him to his ultra academic colleagues with their Victorian attitudes.

L. W. Payne, Jr. however, always judged others by their accomplishments, not their personas. He saw Dobie's earliest writings and was impressed. "My Dad saw in Dobie a diamond in the rough," said Payne's daughter.

Nominally a Methodist, Dobie evolved into a deist, if not an agnostic.[2] Payne, who converted from his Methodist origins to become a Baptist in Austin, was a founder and deacon of The University Baptist Church in Austin. Politically Dr. Payne was a traditional Southern Democrat. Dobie, to put it lightly, was far to the left of Payne. Yet the two men maintained a professional and personal relationship which lasted thirty-one years until Payne's death.

Part of the success of their relationship lay in the fifteen year age difference. When they first met, Payne was forty-one, Dobie twenty-six. Professor Payne became a kind of father figure for

25

Dobie. Payne was the traditional authority figure who tolerated Dobie's artistic manner even when it was so different from his own, as a good father might. Yet also like a good father, Dr. Payne saw the potential in Dobie's early work, encouraged him, and never quit defending Dobie to his conservative colleagues.

While Dr. Payne was casting an eye over young Dobie's manuscripts, the ambitious Dobie recruited Payne to write book reviews for *The Dallas Morning News* "Lit Page." The Lit Page had been organized by Dobie's friend, John H. McGinnis. McGinnis served as a professor at Southern Methodist University and editor of *The Southwest Review*.

The Folklore Society went dormant between 1918 and the spring of 1922 because of World War I. When the Society renewed its work in 1922 Dobie began his active association and became secretary-editor. He became its workhorse and made the Society famous.

Dobie's first issue as editor was Folklore Publication II, 1923. He wrote about "Weather Wisdom of The Texas-Mexican Border." Dr. Payne contributed "One Evening as I Sat Courting" (with music). In all, Dobie would edit Folklore Publications II-XVII. His last issue would appear in 1941.

One of the more popular publications was No. III, a compilation of *Legends of Texas,* published in 1924 and running to 253 pages. It proved a huge success and made Dobie well known in Texas.

The first part of *Legends of Texas* was called "Legends of Buried Treasure and Lost Mines," and served as a base for Dobie's famous novel, *Coronado's Children.*

Part II concerned "Legends of the Supernatural," offering legends about ghosts and devils.

"Legends and Lovers" formed the third section and it included lovers' retreats and places to leap for disappointed lovers. For example, Mount Bonnell, near Austin, was once called Antonett's Leap by early settlers of the Colorado Valley in honor of a distressed maiden who leaped to her death.

Part IV offered legends of pirates and pirate treasures.

The last sections of the *Legends of Texas* dealt with "Legendary Origins of Texas Flowers, Names and Streams," and finally "Miscellaneous Legends" ended the book, detailing such legends as the escapades of outlaw Sam Bass.

*   *   *   *   *

On an impulse, and without even consulting his wife, Dobie accepted an offer to be chairman of the English Department at Oklahoma Agricultural and Mechanical College in 1923.[3]

Running The Texas Folklore Society from Stillwater, Oklahoma, presented obvious problems. Dr. Payne spent much time forwarding folklore business and manuscripts from Austin.

Dobie also helped found The Oklahoma Folklore Society. Thus during his first semester at Oklahoma A&M, (now called Oklahoma State University) Dobie found himself chairman of an English Department that he had thought "in a mess, utterly unorganized," while teaching, writing, gathering folklore, and running two folklore societies.

Dobie had not been in Stillwater even a month when he wrote Payne in late September, 1923, "I am hungry for Texas and our library of Texana." It was a hunger that Dobie would express continually in the next year and a half.

By the end of January, 1924, Dobie was working six to eight hours a day on legends of Texas and feeling more nostalgic for the Lone Star State every day. He wrote Payne, "I want very much to go back to Texas. I was just beginning there in a work that I love. I want the volume of legends to prove something about my fitness too. I hope that it will make Dr. Law reverse his opinion as expressed to me when he said that he did not believe that I had been working."

Dobie and his wife Bertha came down to Austin for a folklore meeting in early May, 1924. The visit boosted Dobie's spirits. He wrote Payne, "I cannot express to you how happy, how glad of life, how eager of existence I was in Austin—and as long as I live I shall associate that happiness, that gladness, that eagerness with my stay in your house . . ."

Dobie and Bertha returned to Stillwater to events that reflect both Dobie's stubbornness and sensitivity. Having been ordered to march at graduation, Dobie and Bertha instead went to a rodeo fifty miles from Stillwater, where they saw actual Indians for the first time. Dobie wrote, "These Indians seem incapable of enjoying modernity as we 'civilized' whites do; they are incapable of seizing drudgery as are the negroes; they are cut off from their old eagle like freedom. I had never realized fully before their tragedy; Sunday I saw their camps, their faces."

Dobie spent the summer of 1924 happily collecting legends of Texas and was in high spirits as he wrote Dr. Payne.

> Aboard the Sunset Limited Railroad
> August 26, 1924
>
> Dear Dr. Payne:
>
> I am on my way to Santa Fe. [From] There I go to Stillwater. Leaving Texas is a tragedy for me. I did work so on the horseback trip into New Mexico. I did better. I went down into the high ranch country of the Nueces. Talk about folklore. I got it this summer . . . we rode all over the country digging. I found two men who proved veritolle [sic] miners of legends; also I garnered a rich sheath of Mexican Cowboy (Vaquero) songs.
>
> What a joy it is to be out gathering lore.
>
> Dr. Payne, I want to thank you for the excellent review you had in *The Saturday Review*. Did you see the review *The Christian Science Monitor* gave us? [Re: Legends of Texas]
>
> Please remember me to Mrs. Payne. I dream every day of being back in Austin.
>
> Sincerely Yours,
> J. FRANK DOBIE

Dobie's spirits dulled, however, after the fall semester in Stillwater. Professionally he had made a major breakthrough with several stories published in *Country Gentleman*, a national magazine which paid very well. Yet Dobie complained that *Country Gentleman* "chipped up my paragraphs into the idiotic fragments that they sprinkle their pages with." This national exposure did not calm his obsession to get back to Texas. "And all the time I am hoping that I shall get a chance to go back to the University, not to teach folk-lore but to teach English, which I know how to teach," he wrote.

At the end of January, 1925, J. Frank Dobie began in earnest his campaign to get himself back to The University of Texas. He turned to Dr. Payne.

Oklahoma A & M
Stillwater
Jan 25, 1925

Dear Doctor Payne

It always heartens me to get a letter from you. . . .

In less than two weeks the Oklahoma Folk-Lore Society, of which I am president, meets, and I am going to spout before it. The secretary resigned, and I have had to make out this program, but I have not hurt myself working as I have no great heart for Oklahoma folk-lore.

It is mostly Indian. Yesterday the most historically inclined of the old settlers of this part of the country had me out to his farm, or ranch, as he calls it. I remained with him all night and we scoured all around the country. The net results of my expedition are two thumb-nail legends—and both of them are of Texas, one of which I had heard before but had forgotten! Absolutely, I believe that Texas has more folk-lore of an imaginative type than any other state in the union.

The main reason that I want the regents to let us have a hundred dollars is that we may secure the services of the University Press. We can do better and cheaper printing there than anywhere else and Wright knows our traditions—traditions of format, etc., I mean.

Dr. Payne, Horn has offered me a professorship at Lubbock. [Texas Tech had recently opened] As I understand him, the pay would be more than I am now getting here and the term of the teaching shorter. However, he can not be definite until the Legislature has acted, I believe. I have been recommended for a raise in salary here. But I loath this place, and I do not want to go out to Lubbock—if I can go to Texas.

This is a long letter. Bear with me for a little longer if you will.

I have worked here for two years now. So far I have grown, not dwarfed. I have taught new courses that made me study in new fields. I have even learned a good many new things in the field of folk-lore. I have been successful as an administrator. I have fought for standards, failing more than fifty percent of some of my classes and fighting a whole guard of tin-horn deans and president who are for more students and fewer flunks. I have sworn not to come back next year, though the oath is secret as yet.

29

I loath administration work. How well do I remember that when nearly two years ago I told Dr. Law one day that I believed I had been studying, researching, as hard as anyone on campus, he replied point-blank that he did not believe me. That reply was typical of the injustice and misunderstanding that drove me from the University of Texas. Because I was what is called a popular teacher it was at once taken for granted that I was a cheap teacher. I was badly in debt. I am out now. I do not ask for anything like the salary I am now drawing. $3000 would be ample for me. But I have started something that seems worthwhile to me, and I can never finish it unless I am where libraries are. There will be no library at Lubbock. Webb wrote me that Barker had turned him over the field of western history; there is a little field of western literature for somebody; I know that field. There are worlds of newspapers that should be gone into in search of more Texas legends. One particular reason why I want to be in Austin is that there I can prepare memorial biographies of Kendall, Taylor, M. E. M. Davis, and one or two other early Texas writers who are deserving and really worth having something definite set down about them. Then I am working on this dictionary of cattle country diction . . . I must have more than 1500 words and phrases recorded—perhaps 2000.

Of course, I do not think that I am necessary to Texas. Nobody is necessary. Stevenson said that Shakespeare might not be worth more than a pound or two of good tobacco; but *comparatively* I can not for the life of me see why the things I have been working on are not worth something in Texas. Did you see Mark Van Doren's article in the *Nation*, December 24, LEGENDS OF TEXAS?

Now, here is the point. You are behind me. Parlin would be behind me. I am confident that if you alone reviewed the matter with Splawn, [UT President] Splawn would do something. I do not know what Sutton had been told. He volunteered to me that he had had more objections to my leaving than to the leaving of any other man, and he volunteered that "We are going to get you back." I think that a little talk by him to Splawn would help. I know that Winkler and Hildebrand have pulled for me. I am willing to go off to study—only I reserve the right to go where I please and to study what I please. I know what kind of milk gives me power and what kind constipates me. If I did not know by now I should be fired out of my profession.

I did not leave Texas merely for money. I want to go back now, and not merely for money. If I had not thought that a leave of absence would surely be given me, I should never have left anyhow, I believe. Well, if you talk to Splawn, please let me know. I feel that it is this year or never.

I tried to get you invited up here for a series of talks before that Oklahoma State Teachers' Association. The committee got the famous Ward of the textbooks. I hear that you are bringing out a new anthology of American literature.

I send you a copy of my article on "Cowboy Songs." The *Country Gentleman* gave me $600 for it and two other articles, one on "The Old Time Trail Drivers" and one on "The Chisholm Trail." The other two have not been published yet. The cowboy songs article was very good before the editors cut out some of the most meaty paragraphs and then sliced the others up into something that resembles bat-droppings. All they did was to make a paragraph of each sentence; the result is idiotic. . . .

Please pardon this lucubration, this "scholarly monograph" on that minor pedagogue, J.F.D. And remember me please to Mrs. Payne. With many, many warm wishes for you both, I am

J. Frank Dobie

P.S. I hope that you are thinking about the anthology of Texas folksongs that we are to get out. It could be made a very large book. We might edit it jointly, if you think that you will be too busy to do it alone, but you are the man to do the collection. Research among certain old Texas publications, notably the *Farm and Ranch*, Dallas Semi-Weekly *Farm News*, etc. would yield a large harvest of folksongs, for departments of such periodicals often publish folk-songs from contributors.

Professor Payne went immediately to work on Dobie's behalf. As Dobie biographer Lon Tinkle observed, "Payne felt Dobie would write books all Texans would be bound to read; and just as genuinely he felt that for Frank to do his best work he needed the discipline and the association of being at The University of Texas."[4] But bringing Dobie back to UT was no sure thing. Payne had a difficult task ahead. He would have to employ some very good diplomatic skills on Dobie's behalf because, as previously explained, Dobie's earthy manner had not endeared him to his colleagues on the Texas faculty. While Payne went to work canvassing his colleagues, he kept Dobie abreast of the developments. Here he made his first report to Dobie.

2104 Pearl Street
Austin, Texas
Feb. 3, 1925

Dear Dobie:

I have sounded out several people here, and the net result is about as follows: The younger adjunct professors will naturally feel it pretty keenly if you go over them to the associateship. There would be less feeling, I think, if you should come in as adjunct professor with top salary. I am sure I shall have to see to it that Cooke goes up to an associateship at all events. I want to see E.M.C. [Clark] raised also, but I should be willing to stand for you first as against him. I rather think that I shall have to concede a little to get the backing I must have in order to put the thing over. I have hopes that I can muster three votes for my minority report. Would you be willing to come as adjunct at all? The highest salary of adjunct would be at $2800, but I think I might get the executive forces to make a special of $3000 in your case, inasmuch as you have a direct offer of more. I believe we could find the money for you if we could smooth out the way. We don't want to have too much opposition here, either in the ranks below or in the committee above. In other words we must have as smooth a sea to sail on together as possible.

I have things pretty well lined up now. I believe, however, that the best way to open the case is for you to write Dr. Law a frank letter, telling him you are thinking of changing your position, that your heart is here, your best chance for the successful pursuit of your speciality is here, and that you would be willing to make some financial sacrifices to come back here. Then write me a letter telling me you have written to Dr. Law and that you know my interest in Folk-lore and Southwestern literature would lead me to want to see you back here at the University. I think it would be easier for me to make the fight on an impersonal basis if one or two letters from you could be made the occasion of calling up the question of getting you back on our campus. If I go and ask for a special meeting to consider your case, I shall at once arouse opposition and be placed on the defensive, as it were. You might also write to Pres. Splawn, asking him if there were any opening other than through the English school whereby you might find a foothold here from which you could do the piece of work that you want to do for Texas. I think I can get Pres. Splawn to send the letter with a favorable comment to the English professors. I believe all he would need would be a hint that would help the cause. I am not sure that it would be wise to involve the President at this stage of the game, however. He would probably want to act as an unbiased umpire in the case. But you can decide whether you think a letter to the president would be wise.

I haven't seen Hildebrand, but Webb, Winkler, Benedict, and others are ready to tear their shirts. Also Lomax said he would do anything he could for you.

To sum up: I am afraid the associateship would cause too much of a hullaboo in the younger group. I think we may be able to manage the $3000. At any rate we can have $2800, and I believe this would be better for you in the long run than to bury yourself for $950 a year more at Lubbock. Your writing would sell better here, and you could do more of it and better—because you would have more material to work on here. I also believe that I can get the $3000 at the adjunct realm in your case. Your special service in Texas Folk-Lore might be frankly made the excuse for an extra hundred or two. I am not weakening on my proposition, but I am trying to smooth out the rough places for your comfort when you get here. I have had to make some compromises in order to get a little more solid backing here. It will be much better if we can split our committee about 3 to 4 rather than 1 to 6.

So write Law a letter and let's start the thing. I think it may take several weeks to work this thing out here. Our committee is very slow at best, and there will be the delayed appropriations bill and the uncertainty of legislative actions as an excuse for delay this year. But I'll try to push the thing to an issue at once. As soon as I get your letter I will ask Law to call a meeting. Make your letter to me fairly full; I may want to read it to the committee. Be sure to put in the point that you are willing to sacrifice in salary to come here. You may mention your offer to Horn, for I rather think Law knows of it or expects it to occur.

Sincerely yours,
L. W. PAYNE, JR.

Dobie exhibited a prolific pen in his own behalf. On February 6,

Dobie wrote at least four long letters, three of them to Payne. Those four letters detailed Dobie's position and feelings.

Oklahoma A & M
Stillwater
February 6, 1925

Dr. L. W. Payne, Jr.
University of Texas
Austin, Texas.

Dear Doctor Payne:

I have been offered a place in the new college at Lubbock at $3750 per year on the basis of nine months of teaching. I am more than eager to get back to the state of Texas, but more than anything in the world I want to return to the University of Texas. Knowing your sympathy for the work I am trying to do in the literature and folk-lore of the West and Southwest, I am writing to you, although I have made formal application to Dr. Law.

The work I have been doing is only begun. If I were put to it I could start the printers tomorrow on a second volume of LEG-ENDS OF TEXAS as large as the volume published last year. It would not be well edited, however, and it would be devoid of much that it should be. I cannot do the work even in literature of the folk without much research. Austin is the only place that I know of where I can do that research. I have other projects in hand also, and all call for research.

Whether or not the work I am doing in the literature and lore of the West and the Southwest is worth doing I must leave to others. I can only say that to me, in this world of shadows where we each pursue so fantastically our several phantoms, it seems as worth-while as nearly anything else. At least the work is having a far felt influence, the evidences of which it is not necessary to state to you.

In my letter to Doctor Law I said that I certainly should not expect $3750 at the University of Texas. I do expect as much as $3000 and I think that I am entitled to an associate-professorship. But I leave those matters to the decision of your committee.

Deeply appreciate of your sympathy for what I am trying to do, I am

Sincerely yours
J. FRANK DOBIE

Stillwater
February 6, 1925

Dear Doctor Payne:

Your letter came today and I am enclosing you herewith copy of my letter to Doctor Law; also I enclose a more formal letter that you may use for campaign purposes. I shall write to President Splawn within a day or so, but I am not sure that the letter I shall write to him had best be spread before the committee, though I do not in the least contemplate saying anything disrespectful of the old guard.

I do not believe that I shall be able to stave Horn off longer than March 1, though I can stave him off that long, I am sure.

I see your point of view with respect to the associate-professorship. Yet, I had never observed before that the English Department was very tender of the feelings of the underlings in making promotions. I came to the University of Texas in 1914, Clark being the only present adjunct professor who was there at that time. The others all came during the war or afterwards. I know that I do not have a degree, [Ph.D.] and I am respectful of that degree, but at the same time I am respectful of my own abilities and I believe that I am worth as much as any of the men.

However, if necessary, I'll come as an adjunct at $3000. The reason that I want an associate professorship is that the rank would allow me to work free. Otherwise, this same fight will have to be gone through with every time I am due a promotion. The necessity I have felt of off-setting my want of the degree has made me work twice as hard as most of the men who have it. I do not say it boastingly, but I am beginning to realize that I can work a great deal more rapidly than most of them also. I am glad that Cooke is in line for promotion. Of the others I know but one who would have any right to kick at my promotion over their heads; that one is Click, and he is too generous to kick. I always thought that Cooke, Click and I were about equals, and the others I considered vastly inferior!

Well, I hate to bother you so much. I hate to bother myself too! No matter what comes, I have enjoyed long the feeling of growing power within me and I know that I have not reached the zenith of my accomplishments. Dr. Payne, I actually think that I can write someday a history of The Chisholm Trail that will take its place beside the *Oregon Trail*. I'll be glad when the time comes that I shall

35

not feel the necessity of singing my own praises. You will be gladder.

With a thousand indebtedness, I am

Sincerely yours

J. FRANK DOBIE

I say that I will take a $3000 adjunctship. At the same time I think that I deserve a rank higher, and also I wonder if I am putting my head into a sack. But I have got to have those libraries. I am paralyzed without them.

(Payne's copy of Dobie's letter to Law)

February 6, 1925

Dr. R. A. Law
Chairman of the Department of English
University of Texas
Austin, Texas

. . . It would be superfluous for me to say anything of my teaching ability. However, I think it is not amiss to review something of the work I have done since I left the University. My regular schedule here has been nine hours of teaching per week. I have taught one class of advanced composition, Shakespeare, American Literature, and, for one term, Contemporary Drama (about which I make no pretensions of knowing anything); this spring and summer I propose teaching a short course in Chaucer. These new fields have forced me to do a considerable amount of studying, and, while our library is lamentably lacking, I have found in it more than I could learn. What I am trying to say is that I have grown somewhat in knowledge.

In wisdom I do not know how I have fared. I have certainly had experiences in exercising it. Last year I had to devote a great deal of time to organizing a department that was chaotic and to trying to standardize the work of certain lax and incompetent teachers. Happily, I have a rather hardy constitution, and I found that by working until one o'clock in the morning I was able to get some things done outside of routine duties. This year our staff of teachers has been much bettered, and much less of my time has been consumed in executive work,—a work that I dislike.

Like many other men, I am not teaching English merely for

money. But I believe that it would never be possible for me to put my full heart into teaching at any other place than the University of Texas. My head is as dependent as my heart on this one place in the universe. For three years and a half now I have worked hard in the field of folk-lore and literature of Texas and the Southwest. I have done some work that certain men of judgment over the country have called worth doing. I want to continue that work. I cannot continue it and do it well without diligent research in the libraries at Austin.

I know very definitely what I want to do, and I hope that I shall not suffer the imputation of immodesty when I say that I am peculiarly fitted to do the work I have mapped out for myself. I want to continue my work in folk-lore, particularly legends, and I want to make studies in the literary and social backgrounds—I find it hard to separate the two—of the Southwest and the West. It may not be amiss to say that I see a particularly fertile field in the diction of the Southwest. For several years now I have been compiling a kind of dictionary of the locutions peculiar to this section of country, especially those that have been and that are being used in the ranching areas. . . .

> With best wishes, I am
> Respectfully yours
> [J. FRANK DOBIE]

> Stillwater
> February 6, 1925

Dear Dr. Payne:

I have decided not to write to President Splawn. It would probably look better if I did not. If old Doctor Sutton, Winkler, Hildebrand, and Battle would talk to him their talk would be much more effective than my letter.

I had forgot Doctor Battle as an ally. He is one and a strong one. I do not know how much action he would take, but I do know that he would do something and that he would be found sympathetic.

Thus, I leave you sole general. Whatever comes, I'll be in debt to you the rest of my life. Perhaps in my formal letter to you I should not have mentioned an associate-professorship and $3000. Yet, I do not know why I should not. The more I think of it, the more tragic it seems to me it would be to go out to libraryless Lubbock; the more heavenly it would be to be back in libraried Austin. Well, I do

not see how they are going to get around the wide effect LEGENDS
OF TEXAS has had; but the evidence of my work in folk-lore is
more patent to me in letters never seen by anybody else than it is in
printed words.

Why, Dr. Payne, you, Miss Burch, myself, and a few others could
make of the Texas Folk-Lore Society a power nearly as great as the
Texas Historical Association. We have established something of a
system in selling—Miss Burch has. I propose for her a salary. Then
I see us reprinting now and then some old book meaty with the
exposition of folk-lore and educating the people of the state to read
it and value it. We can do it. I have my mind on two such books to
be reprinted. Our Society is surpassing the Texas Poetry Society as
a power for creating interest in our own life and literature. We have
made but a beginning, if—.

Well, I have a bad cold and have just swallowed the last drop of
Mexican tequila that I brought up here from the Texas border . . .

Sincerely yours,

J. FRANK DOBIE

Despite Payne's vigorous efforts, Dobie lost the first round, as
expected. On February 12, the English committee voted 4-2 not to
offer Dobie the associate professorship. Having anticipated this,
Payne had on hand a minority report which he immediately filed
in dissent. It stated that not to bring Dobie back to UT would be a
great loss, that Dobie's book, *Legends of Texas,* had already brought
great prestige to UT, that the interest in folk-lore would probably
follow Dobie if he worked at another institution in Texas. And appealing to a university under political pressure to keep budgets
down, Payne said Dobie was willing to come back to UT at a considerable financial sacrifice.

As seen in Dobie's letters to Dr. Payne on February 6, Dobie had
been offered a job at Texas Tech in Lubbock, which had just formed.
In the following exchange of letters Dobie revealed his feelings
about going to Lubbock, as compared to the possibility of returning to The University of Texas. In return correspondence, Payne's
letters provided Dobie with the most intimate details of Payne's behind the scenes diplomacy.

Stillwater
February 20, 1925

Dear Doctor Payne:

. . . I know that you are doing all that you can do, and I am not in the least worrying over the delay. . . .

I have in mind to write Doctor Law also, but one doubt comes up. I know from various sources the way Dr. Callaway has of winning his case by putting things off. If he knew that I had only a short time to make my decision in I believe that he would not hesitate to take advantage of the situation in order to down me. I may be wrong. If you think that it would be the best policy for me to write to Dr. Law and tell him that I must know by March 1, then please wire me at my expense. You can just wire "Write the letter" or something like that. As I wrote the other day, I received a very cordial letter from Dr. Law.

I might worm out of Dr. Horn a four or five days more of time. One thing is certain: I would not stay here another year for all the salaries in Oklahoma. If Texas does not want me, then Lubbock is the next step. I feel strangely confident, however, about the University situation. Romeo's "Bosom's lord sat lightly in his throne" also!

I hope that you are fishing this warm day. With a thousand good wishes, I am

Sincerely yours,
J. Frank Dobie

P.S. Of course in my first letter to Doctor Law I told him that I was being pressed for time, but I have no definite limit.

The University of Texas
Feb. 21, 1925

Dear Dobie:

We have had a battle royal over the problem of your coming back. I made a minority report with one vote supporting me all the way, and two votes going to $2800 adjunctship. The Dean and President called us to a conference of two hours, where it was all fought over again. The Dean recommended the minority report to Pres. and he has now taken it to the legislative committee, and he thinks it will go through. It is for three associateships for English at $3000 each, or if this is possible, associateship for Cooke and 2 $2800 ad-

39

junctships for you and E. M. Clark. I think the first recommendation will go to the legislature. There it may be stopped. I told Pres. Splawn that I feared we would lose you if we did not go to the higher figure and rank. It was the devil of a fight.

Please don't give me away for letting out what is still a secret so far as the English dept. is concerned. In fact, please don't let it be known that I have communicated with you so intimately and fully. It is entirely ex cathedra and nonethical according to the view of some.

With best wishes.
Sincerely yours,
L. W. PAYNE, JR.

Dobie's letter of February 20 had just reached Payne when he wrote this letter on Washington's birthday.

2104 Pearl Street
Austin, Texas
Feb. 22, 1925

Dear Dobie:

I had already mailed you a letter which crossed your special delivery, so I did not think it necessary to write you. A letter to Law would do no good now. I had a little talk with Pres. Splawn yesterday, and I got the following general information from him. Benedict recommended three $3000 places or one $3000 and two $2800 adjunct professorships for Cooke, Clark and yourself in the order named. Dr. Splawn said that he felt sure he could get the regents to guarantee the last set of figures—He said that under circumstances, both financial and academic, the best he could do for you would be the top adjunctship. I argued that we might lose you on this basis, and that I thought the state would be the gainer in every way to pay you $3000 here rather than $3750 in Lubbock. He agreed and wanted to make the offer, but he felt that the compromise was necessary on account of others here on the ground. He also said that in the face of the opposition to your elevation above other men here, it might be three or four years before you could look for promotion. In other words you would have to take your chance along with others, and you know how slow promotion here is with our internal problems and external legislative uncertainty. I wanted you to know the full facts so that you can make your decision intelligently, so I asked Pres. Splawn if I might write you the above facts in confidence. He said that I ought to inform you of the exact situation.

So the situation is up to you. I have made a hard fight, and in a way I have won; but I shall look upon the whole thing as a Cadmean victory unless I see you actually on our campus. I shall be perfectly satisfied with such a victory, however, if you decide that you cannot accept the $2800 adjunctship. I should not blame you in the least. In fact, if I were in your place I think that $950 would tip the balance toward West Texas. However you might take into consideration the chance for a summer term here. Nothing was said about summer work, but under ordinary circumstances you would have one term each summer if you so desired. Then you could count on some lecture work here, and certainly your writing would command more attention from here than from West Texas. The whole problem is whether you are willing to go to West Texas for two or three years of organization work without the library facilities or come here and go right on with your present projects. This is your chance to get back on our staff. I seriously doubt whether you would ever have a chance to come on the English faculty here again. You might get back on some special arrangement with Comparative Literature or something like that, but I doubt if the English door can ever be pried open again under present conditions. One of my colleagues suggested that if you come to Lubbock we might call you here in a year or two, but I consider that a remote contingency and so said. I believe it is now or never so far as this particular job is concerned.

I want to say that there has been the warmest personal regard and commendation expressed by all concerned. If you were considered on your personal qualities you could be elected to be President of the United States, if we are to take protestations at face value. And I think these expressions are sincere. There is a difference of opinion as to your ability as a writer and as to the value of the kind of scholarship which you practice, but there is no differences of opinion as to your personal charm and magnetism. If you come, you will be welcomed cordially by all, but of course there are some who will think you ought not to come under the circumstances, that is, that would not come if placed in the same position as you are. Still that is a matter for you to decide and if you are ready to fight for your right to pursue scholarly happiness in your own way you are clearly within your constitutional rights. There will be no personalities here, I think, and I am confident that time and your accomplishments will indicate the justice of your call to this field.

So to sum up I will say that the decision must be entirely yours. I shall be satisfied with whatever that decision is. If you go to Lubbock, we will just work on as we have done for the past two years. If you come here, the problem of the development of the Texas Folk-Lore Society will be simplified. I shall feel that I have made a good fight for the cause, whatever the outcome may be, and as you know there is some satisfaction in the consciousness of having done one's best. Don't consider my feelings to be involved, for frankly they are not. [The preceding sentence should not be taken literally. Payne certainly was emotionally involved. He wanted Dobie to return very much.] I can easily put myself in your place; and as I say, if I were in your place I should be greatly tempted to take the bigger salary. You may see that your work here would make you happier, even on less money, and yours must be the decision on that matter. . . .

. . . we won't worry over the folklore business until we get the other issue settled. The Regents meet today, and I imagine you will get some sort of offer within the next two or three days. I hope this letter will be in your hands when the offer comes.

Sincerely yours,
L. W. PAYNE, JR.

Dobie's stubbornness surfaced in his February 23 letter to Payne. Maybe he would not go back to The University of Texas after all.

Stillwater, Oklahoma
February 23, 1925

Dear doctor Payne:

Your interesting letter came today. I am positively ashamed of myself that you should be battling for me so royally, though, objectively, I believe that I am worth the fight. Well, just for the fun I should like to have heard some of the arguing. Rest assured that I shall not tell a soul, except my wife, of how you have taken me into confidence.

I hope that the offer comes for $3000 and associateship. Otherwise I think that I should doubt the advisability of going, for after such a hard fight it is clear that any other advancement could be obtained only through irregular methods, and I should not be content to rest a mere adjunct. I know that I can go up elsewhere, and while, as I have often said, Texas is the only place that my heart and head turn to, something besides the privilege of being there is required.

I did not know the legislature any longer fixed every item of expenditure. If the matter had to be threshed out in the legislature I could play a merry game there if I had a mind to take a hand in it. But I have not, and so there's an end to that. I'll have to wire Mr. Horn yes or no next Sunday.

I had no idea that this LEGENDS OF TEXAS was going to bring me into such notoriety. I had two requests for "something" today from minor publications. Bobbs Merrill want me to write a book, but I'll consider a while before I make any engagement with them. I have two articles on New Mexico (and Nueces River) folk-tales that I am about ready to send to the *Century.* Wish me luck.

Sincerely your friend,
J. Frank Dobie

Letters crossed in the mails and there may be some confusion in understanding Dobie's attitude change in his February 25 letter. However, two days after his February 23 letter, he had calmed down. What calmed him the most was certainly Payne's February 22 letter, which had just reached Stillwater, announcing that Dobie should get an offer from UT in a few days.

Stillwater, Oklahoma
February 25, 1925

Dear Doctor Payne:

Your last letter came today and I am overwhelmed at the audacity and generosity of your battle for me. No offer has come to me as yet, but from your letter I judge that it will come within a day or two. I shall accept it.

Should I go to Lubbock, I should go at best, for the future of this life; I should go as a wage earner. My theory—no matter what the practice—of life is that one had better live during the present. I can live the present in Austin, and I do not distrust the future. My wife, too, wants to live in Austin, and we should both be much happier there. . . .

I am glad there are no hard feelings about the matter. Because a majority of the professors voted against me I feel absolutely no inclination not to come. Some of them owe their elevation to executive action over Dr. Callaway's protest, I understand, and I had as soon think of them as imposters rather than myself! With no idea of comparing myself to Shakespeare, I am very sure that if one or two of them were suddenly to meet that writer's works without the guidance and tradition of centuries to guide them, they would see nothing in them. Dr. Payne, the lack of literary sense in the average American Ph.D. professor of English is most amazing.

I don't think I'll ever teach in summer school again. Nobody teaches summer school for any reason except a monetary one. On a purely commercial basis I can make more money doing something else than I can in summer school. I do not believe, however, that what I write would *sell* any better from the University of Texas than it would from Stillwater, Lubbock, Kyle, Pflugerville, or any other place, excepting, of course, something required in academic circles. Their academic prestige means much.

You have put me under lasting obligation to you. I shall do my best to uphold your judgment. The victory you have won will give you strength, too, and I rejoice at that. . . .

> Wishing you much, I am
> Sincerely yours,
> J. FRANK DOBIE

Again, the crossing of letters caused some anxiety. When writing the following letter on February 27, Payne had just received Dobie's letter of February 23, in which Dobie had suggested that he might not accept an offer from UT.

> The University of Texas
> Feb. 27, 1925

Dear Dobie:

Your letter came yesterday, and early today I got a conference with Pres. Splawn and Dean Benedict. I read your letter to them and told them I feared you would decline the offer of $2800 and rank of adjunct. Naturally you would not want to come in the face of the opposition of the committee. I was directed by Pres. Splawn to say that under the present unsettled condition of the University finances, the best he could do would be to guarantee you a $2800 adjunctship. He authorizes me to offer you this as coming from him. I asked him if he could make any promises as to your future promotion. He declined to make any definite promises, for that would be beyond his power, but he and Dean Benedict both agreed that so long as they were in office your case would be reviewed independently of the English committee's recommendations. In other words you will not be entirely dependent on recommendations from the English professors. This, they said, was only fair and just in view of the way in which your appointment has been brought about.

I want you to come on back and build up your special field of interest here at the University. I feel sure that you will make a place for yourself and that you will be advanced as soon as an opportunity offers. The outlook here is doubtful because of legislative interference and lack of full appropriations, but I have assurances from present authorities that if fortune favors the University your interests will be duly taken care of. So while there are no definite promises or assurances, there is the satisfaction of knowing that your case will not rest entirely on the attitude of the English professors.

I leave the whole matter to your discretion. I don't want you to come for my sake. I feel that I have merely done my duty as I saw it; and if I don't succeed in getting you back on the campus, I shall take what satisfaction there is in the feeling that I at least did my "durndest."

I'll ask the President to have Dr. Law send you a telegram tomorrow. In the meantime I think I shall telegraph you to await the coming of this letter—which I shall send as a special delivery.

Sincerely yours,
L. W. PAYNE, JR.

The happy conclusion to Payne's maneuvering for Dobie is best described in Dobie's jubilant letter which he wrote Payne as soon as he accepted the offer to return to The University of Texas.

Stillwater
February 28, 1925

Dear Doctor Payne:

There is at least one happy couple in flat Stillwater tonight. We are going back to Austin! Your special delivery letter came this afternoon. About the same time a telegram came from Doctor Law offering me adjunctship at $2800. I have written him an acceptance; I have written Mr. Horn a declination, at the same time suggesting that J. P. Simmons would be a good man for the place. I have also written Simmons urging him to get in touch with Mr. Horn. [Simmons accepted a position at Baylor University.] That is a good place at Lubbock; I believe that Horn is going to hold up a decent standard.

I am very sure that you did "your derndest," and, all things considered, the result seems to me pretty derned good. We can live on the salary; I shall no longer be at the very tail of the lion; and—perhaps it is a sign of age—the sense of settled security will be a source of strength that I have never experienced. I cannot express to you the joy that comes from the prospect of leaving this flat, colorless, mid-western atmosphere together with the petty time consumers that make up the round of such an executive position as I have endured. If all my tequila were not gone and if my wife were of a bibulous nature I should insist on our getting drunk this very night. If there is any enemy that you want murdered, any shoes that you want cleaned, or any other small matter that you wish tended to, kindly ask me, and I shall respond.

I shall never mention to anyone the assurance that President Splawn and Dean Benedict conveyed to me through you. You have spent an immense amount of time on this business. I hope now that you can rest and work in peace.

With best wishes always, I am

Sincerely yours,
J. Frank Dobie

And so in the year 1925, with Dobie back in Austin, the written record between the two men disappears. Now in the same town and in the same department of the University, Dobie and Payne met and worked frequently on folklore.

It was five years later, in 1930, that Dobie thanked Payne for his help in bringing him back to Texas. Dobie did it in a quiet way, but in a way Payne cherished most. In Payne's copy of *Coronado's Children*, perhaps Dobie's most famous book, Dobie scribbled a note thanking Dr. Payne for fighting for him and finding him at The University of Texas "the only proper lying-in place in the world."

CHAPTER FIVE

A Cummings Critic

A question asked many times about literary critics is if they themselves tried to write creative literature. The answer in Dr. Payne's case is yes; when in his middle twenties during the 1890s he wrote short stories. In writing the fictional pieces, he used the excesses of Victorian prose of the time and his short stories did not prove successful. As far as is known, he never attempted to write poetry.

Having experienced the frustrations of attempting to write creative fiction, Payne developed a sympathy for the struggles of the poet and novelist. Payne's experience as a failed short story writer also developed in him a patience for the first jottings of the young, insecure, inexperienced writers. Payne recognized the rough cuts of future greatness in the early writings of Stark Young and J. Frank Dobie. Yet above all, Payne's failing as a creative writer developed an insatiable curiosity to understand *how* and *why* the creative process worked. This insatiable curiosity, obviously partly propelled by Payne's innate intelligence which was considerable, predated his brief attempts at writing short stories. But the sobering experience of actually trying to write stories produced in Payne an understanding and humility that helped make him a great critic, an interpreter of literature to students and adults alike.

In the first few decades of the twentieth century, American literature was considered inferior to English literature and consequently little taught in American universities. Professor Payne became one of the first teachers to actually specialize in teaching American literature. Professor Payne admired Mark Twain tremendously and became an expert on the great American satirist. Yet the old masters like Twain did not hold the only interest for Professor Payne. He developed a curiosity about the emerging

radical writers of the new century. The young American writer
who most excited Dr. Payne by the second decade of the new century was e. e. cummings, the brilliant poet who imposed his presence upon the American literary scene just after World War I. Professor Payne was one of the first critics to gauge the greatness of
the poet who remains famous today mostly because of his odd
punctuation and omission of capital letters in his poetry.

Cummings impressed Professor Payne with poetry, though unconventional, "rich with metaphors, brilliant pictures, and imaginative power and insight." Dr. Payne declared Cummings the
most richly endowed with genius of the poets emerging in the
World War I era.

Dr. Payne became one of the first critics to take notice of
Cummings' painting as well as his poetry. And that, as some of Cummings' letters to Payne show, pleased the young New Englander
greatly.

In order to understand Cummings, Dr. Payne had to study the
unconventional patterns of the poetry and learn about modern
painting, with which Cummings deeply involved himself. Despite
his unconventional lines, Cummings' art was deeply rooted in
tradition[1] and Professor Payne felt comfortable with that. Cummings wrote poetry of great emotion, resembling in some ways
Elizabethan lyricists and nineteenth century romantics,[2] the very
kind of poetry which won Payne's heart as a boy. Concerning his
unorthodox punctuation, Cummings said he used the lower case
"i" because English was the only language with which he was familiar that capitalized the personal pronoun, first case.[3] For Cummings this odd punctuation in fact had a visual connotation.[4]
Cummings' broken lines and words offered a sense of visual
structure similar to that of a painting. The devices also high-
lighted pause and emphasis, and underscored the meaning of
words and lines. Cummings intended that meanings develop as
the reader's mind slowed in its journey through the poem and became forced to go back and forth, hence hitting upon the meanings in an immediate moment of perception.[5]

Cummings' contemporary Wallace Stevens observed that poets
often turned to the literature of painting for a discussion of per-

sonal problems. The main concept which Cummings and his contemporaries assimilated stemmed from Cézanne, who believed that a picture existed as a self-contained organism. The picture existed as itself and not as a picture of something else, or about something else which it approximated.[6]

Dr. Payne judged correctly in taking Cummings' painting seriously. In fact, Cummings, who maintained that his work in these mediums complemented each other, painted more than he wrote.[7] Cummings' poetry in *Dial* appeared first in 1920. His popular book *The Enormous Room*, about his imprisonment in World War I, was published in 1922. Yet Cummings had exhibited his paintings since 1919.[8] Cummings painted in the day and wrote at night.

Professor Payne's interest in Cummings' work went beyond a critic's curiosity. He had to explain Cummings to his students at The University of Texas. And when Professor Payne wanted to know something about a writer still living, he did not consult other critics first. He wrote the writer directly and asked his questions. In late July, 1925, Dr. Payne began outlining a lecture on Cummings for the approaching fall term. Dr. Payne also planned to write an article about Cummings and to include him in *Selections from American Literature*, an anthology Payne was writing. He wrote Cummings with questions and comments. Cummings responded immediately.

4 Patchin Place
August 3, 1925

Dear Professor Payne:

I have your letter of July 27.

I should be most happy to cooperate with you in obtaining coloured slides of my "abstract" paintings, should the occasion offer.

Concerning the aesthetic points which you mention: all (including "abstract" art) are clearly discussed in Willard Huntington *Wright's Modern Painting* (subtitle: Its Tendency and Meaning)— John Lane Co., MCMXV—and I suggest that you enlighten your audience via this book, which is written for people without experience in modern painting.

I am glad that you are aware of my predilection for *movement*. Before all, one is alive or not alive; if intensely alive, one is possibly an "artist."

So as to particulars: there is no "storey book" of any of the paintings—or if there is, I am unable to reveal it. I have drawn since I was able to hold a pencil; that is (so to speak) that. I visited Robin Hood (near Stonington, whence John Marin lifted some of his excellent motifs) last year, but only Freud knows why the sources in question "attracted" me. The nuptuous water-color was painted, if I remember correctly, in France (probably at Pornic, in 1923) and the motivation of its "abnormalities" will, I trust, be clear to you after you have indulged in Wright's chapters on Cézanne, Picasso, and synchronism (not that I am a synchronist or any other—ist, my work being—whatever it may or may not be—mine.)

The bust is a portrait of myself by Gaston Lachaise. It was constructed a few months ago.

Scofield Thayer and W. C. Blum, in the Dial, have defined many "eccentricities" of my technique-in-writing and have explained the causes (E.g. capitals for emphasis). I regret that I have no file of The Dial, so am unable to say which numbers contain the criticisms referred to; but I'm sure you'll have no difficulty in locating them.

Your program sounds very interesting and I wish you success in a certainly periculous undertaking. If my letter appears to you uncommunicative, you may be sure that the inability to furnish statistics, interpretations, etc. is in no wise related to my attitude, which is enthusiastic.

Sincerely yours,
e. e. cummings

P.S. If this will help—

I consider El Greco the greatest painter who ever lived; Picasso the greatest living painter, Lachaise the greatest living sculptor, and Stravinski the greatest living musician.

c

Professor Payne wrote and delivered his lecture to his English charges. Afterwards, he sent a copy of the lecture to Cummings, who commented on it.

4 Patchin Place Sunday [nd]

Dear Professor Payne—

Thanks very much for your letter, enclosing the outline of your lecture. (I'm returning the outline.) I'm glad the lecture was successful! It sounds to me as if a considerable number of sleep-walkers had found themselves wideeyed on the front porch of the nth storey of ignorance, thanks to your strenuous efforts . . .

I enjoyed greatly your synopsis. The Wright book seems to have been of use, and for this I'm thankful; since the fact of undermining the habit of notseeing is a past one, and the accomplishments of that task an extraordinary triumph.

I note these minor mistakes (biographical): I was imprisoned at La Ferte- Mace (Orue) with perhaps 3 score or 3½ s. "unfortunates" (unless the E.R. otherwise states: it being accurate)—after serving in the Norton Harjes Ambulance Corps as a volunteer (with the French Army): I was released in December and returned to America immediately: in America I was drafted (Thank you for noting this!!) and sent to Camp Devins, Massachusetts, where I remained 6 months until (honorably) discharged—hence I did not serve in the "American overseas forces."

That you have stressed my painting as you did gives me the most pleasure of all—

Yours
cummings

One of Professor Payne's most insightful reviews was published in December, 1925 in the *Longhorn Magazine* of The University of Texas. The subject was Cummings, the mood was euphoric.

"E. E. Cummings, Painter and Poet"
by L. W. Payne, Jr.

Literature is a continuous stream—a growing, going thing—and new voices are continually being lifted up, calling loudly for attention, appealing for a hearing. The "new poets" of the second decade of the twentieth century are already becoming the "older poets." Some half dozen of them have now been definitely classified as "major," and their works have been put in the anthologies and are being studied in the schools, so that these poets are already ticketed under the spurious modern title of "classics." But there is always a group of "younger" aspirants who come forward to try new forms and media.

Of these new poets the most daring, the most radical, and in my judgment the most richly endowed with poetic genius is Edward Estlin Cummings. He is both a radical painter and a radical poet; and hence to comprehend or understand his work in either of these branches of art one must study his productions in the other.

Young Cummings appears to be a man of remarkable vitality. I am rather of the opinion that Mr. Cummings is one of those strange, incomprehensible, anomalous beings that appear now and again on earth, not to be thoroughly analyzed or understood, but to be frankly accepted and classified under the mysterious title of genius. He is the most alive and original writer that I have read in a long time. He has himself read widely, and he seems to have the Macaulay faculty of remembering everything he reads; yet the evidence in his works plainly shows that he has absorbed rather than imitated other books. Being endowed by nature with the artistic instinct, he had to find some avenue of artistic expression. He has drawn, he says, ever since he could hold a pencil in his hand, and he seems restless unless he has either a pencil or a pen in his hand. He is always drawing pictures, whether in words or in lines and shades and colors.

It is impossible without the aid of ample illustrations to give anything like an adequate idea of Mr. Cummings' drawings and pictures. A number of his line drawings have been reproduced in the *Dial* from time to time, and I have examined seven or eight photographs of his pictures in oil and water colors. Although he refuses to be classified, I think he belongs nearest to the latest school of futurists known as synchronists. However, he disclaims the connection, saying, "not that I belong to the synchronists or any other—ist, my work being—whatever it may or may not be—mine." It is interesting to note that Mr. Cummings esteems El Greco as the greatest painter who ever lived; Picasso the greatest living painter; Lachaise the greatest living sculptor; and Stravinski the greatest living musician.

In order to understand the radical forms of modern art, one must read the dicta of the best critics and try to apply what the critics say to the works of the artists themselves. Such books as Wright's *Modern Painting: Its Tendencies and Meaning* and Marriott's *Modern Movements in Painting* will give one an insight into what modern art means. If one will read these books attentively, one will soon realize that through all the schools—the Impressionists, the Neo-Impressionists, the Cubists, the Futurists, the Vorticists, the Dadaists, and the Synchronists—the general tendency in modern painting is more and more toward abstraction in art. The painters no longer attempt to imitate or reproduce nature realistically, but rather to reproduce the artist's personal impression of the object. From this stage we move on to the Post-Impressionists, who attempt not to reproduce their own impressions but rather the elemental nature and internal fabric as presented directly to the human mind and imagination. They strive after esthetic ecstacy by appealing directly, without the intervention of recognizable forms, to the intellect and imagination. In fact, they distort nature, if necessary, to gain this effect. The result is that the uninformed think the artists have all gone "dippy" and no longer paint things which ordinary individuals in their normal minds can recognize. Some of the extremely radical artists say frankly that they do not care to present recognizable subject-matter, but rather pure abstractions, so that the emotional and imaginative natures of the spectators may be aroused in their pure and unobstructed qualities. Imitative art, they say, is the lowest and elemental form of reproductive art. The photographer can beat all the artists when it comes to the mechanical reproduction of nature as it really is. We do not demand imitation in music; why, then, should we demand it in painting or poetry or the other arts? If a musician writes a composition on a storm or on Niagara Falls, he may give us a few imitative chords or phrases here and there, but his musical composition as a whole is nothing like a storm or a waterfall. The musician strives to catch the inner spirit of his subject and translates into sound the emotion it produces. So must the painter translate the essence, the dynamism, if you please, of his subject into color, design, drawing.

Now, when we come to apply all these modern notions of art to poetry, what do we get? The medium of the poet is words rhythmically arranged so as to produce an esthetic on the mind or the intellect, but on the emotions and the imagination as well. It is not at all necessary, then, to understand what you read in the new poetry. (To most of us this is a comforting assurance.) All that you need to do is yield yourself to the beauty of the artist's conception, to the soothing rhythm of the cadences, whether you understand the words or not. The words are beautiful in themselves if artistically arranged to produce a desired esthetic effect. Try to exercize your imagination and emotional nature without the intervention of your intellect, and thus enjoy the elemental esthetic values of the vowel and consonantal combinations in musical and rhythmically pleasing patterns. Those of us who have been trained in the old ways of trying to understand what the poet is saying are absolutely and positively—or as Cummings playfully puts it, *abslatively* and *posolutely*—non-plussed when we try to read this new poetry in its more radical forms. We cannot rid ourselves of preconceived notions of what poetry is or what a poet is supposed to do when he writes verse. We are not trained in the ways of abstraction and esthetic and imaginative detachment. We think the poet's business is to give us pleasure by repeating well-worn thoughts and to soothe us with babyish rockings of simple rhythms, easy cadences, and familiar rimes at the ends of the lines. When the modern poet tells us to forget all this, discard our preconceived notions, and detach ourselves from our lifelong habits, we are utterly unable to do so, and hence we miss the esthetic message, the imaginative thrill designed by the poet. I, for one, am too old-fashioned, I think, ever to be able to appreciate fully the newer forms of art. But I am willing to learn; in fact, I am anxious to become informed. I don't want to be an old fogy or to be left behind as a castaway or a has-been. Like everybody else who has any life in him, I want to know what is going on in the world. And so I read the modern poetry with an open mind, listen to the new music with an attentive ear, look at the modern pictures earnestly and intently with the eye of one who wants to see, even if I can only half-intelligently guess what it is all about. Another thing I have learned to do is to take the new art seriously. It is perfectly natural for one who does not understand or respond to a thing to say that it has no meaning, to affirm that the artists themselves don't know what they are trying to do and are simply making monkeys of an ignorant and gullible public. This is unfair and unsportsmanlike. Let us at least attribute sincerity and honesty of purpose to the modern artists. Let us at least give them credit for striving courageously to advance their several acts to a higher plane. Whether they succeed or not must be left to the verdict of posterity, but we can certainly give them credit for heroic and sincere intention.

Now, when we come to examine Mr. Cummings as a poet, we find that he looks upon words as a musician does sounds or a painter colors. He thinks that a creative poet has as much right to handle freely his medium, words, as any other artist has to handle the medium of his art freely. He mixes and manipulates his words as a painter mixes and manipulates his colors. He discards all the conventional devices in printing poetry and undertakes to arrange his words, dispose his capitals, and manipulate his punctuation and spacing just as he pleases, without submitting to the tyranny of any set of conventional rules. Why shouldn't he? Surely conventions are not binding on the creative artist. For example, he rarely or never uses a capital at the beginning of a line of poetry, or the pronoun I, or for a proper name even unless he thinks the capital necessary to give emphasis or weight to the word. And he is as likely to print a capital in the middle or at the end of a word as at the beginning. The whole question with him is, does the consonant or the vowel need emphasis; if so, let it be capitalized. Similarly with punctuation marks; if he wants to put a comma or a period or both in the middle of a word or at the beginning of a line, he does it. In his more radical verse he uses very few punctuation marks, and among those he uses the parenthesis which seems to be his favorite, and at times uses it in the most unexpected situations. Words become as maleable in his hands as clay in the hands of a molder. He breaks them up, readjusts them, or telescopes them at will. If he speaks of a pair of playmates he calls them "eddieandbill" or "bettyandisbel" just as one would pronounce the names in rapid speech. He may separate a word by printing one syllable in one line and another in the next line without a hyphen or any other ligature. Sometimes he even forms whole series of lines with the broken elements of a polysyllable. For example, when he wants the reader to emphasize each syllable, to pause, as it were, for the space of a whole cadence on a single sound, he will string out the word over several lines, as in the following poem:

i was considering how
within a night's loose
sack a star's
nibbling in-

fin
  -i-
     tes-
i
  -mal-
  ly devours

darkness the
hungry star
which
will e
-ven-
-tu-
 al
  -ly jiggle
  the bait of
  dawn and be jerked

  into
  eternity. when over my head a
  shooting
  star
  Bur   s
        (t
             into a stale shriek
like an alarm-clock)

Here, as I interpret him, the poet wants his reader to speak the syllables of *infinitesimally* and *eventually* in a slow, emphatic, tense, high-keyed tone, and so he gives a full line to each syllable. The peculiar form of the printing gives the reader a hint as to the exact intonation, the elocutionary or impressionistic effect desired. Similarly at the end of the poem the breaking up of the word *burst* is suggestive of the action implied. But this erratic form of printing is not all there is to the poem. What we have is an impressionistic study of a deeply contemplative or reflective mood suddenly broken by some unexpected occurrence. Imagine yourself looking at a twinkling star on a dark night. You are thinking of what the star is doing, conceiving it in some grotesque figure of speech, say of a mouse infinitesimally nibbling at a piece of cheese representing the darkness, a hungry mouse which will eventually jiggle the bait of the trap and be jerked into eternity, as the star is blotted out by the light of day. Suddenly there blazes over your head a shooting-star, like the brazen crash of an alarm-clock which wakes you from a sound sleep early in the morning. Such an impression could only be adequately suggested by a peculiar printing of words, such as we have here. The stringing out of *infinitesimally* and *eventually* indicates the slow process of passage of time, and the anomalous printing of *burst* with an initial capital and the separation or "*bursting*" of the final consonants with the unexpected interposition of a parenthesis has the effect of bringing you suddenly back to earth.

Or take another impressionistic study of the brilliant coloring of an evening sky just at sunset.

```
        the
             sky
                      was
        can        dy      lu
        minous
                    edible
        spry
             pinks shy
        lemons
        greens        coo     l   choc
        olate
        s.

          un    der,
          a     lo
        co
        mo
             tive      s   pout
                             ing
                               vi
                                o
                              lets
```

Here the syllables are scattered over the page like the colorings of the sunset sky. The poet conceives the sky as a dish of vari-colored candies, while beneath, the locomotive is spouting a column of dark blue smoke. There are rimes, and near-rimes, and alliteration, and onamatapoetic or suggestive word combinations to give a pleasing lyric effect: *sky-spry-shy-vi, lo-co-mo-o, candy-edi, lu-coo; luble chocolates-violets; cool-choc, lemons-cool-late-lo-lets.* The syllables of the last words are printed so as to suggest the sounds of the engine, and the stringing out of the last phrase simulates the movement of the column of smoke. Only a sympathetic reading aloud of the oddly arranged syllables can bring out the full beauty of this impressionistic lyric. As luck would have it, I was driving along the Bull Creek road the day after I recited this poem in a public reading recently, and the whole picture presented in the lyric was realized with startling accuracy in the actual setting of the sunset sky. The sun had disappeared beyond Mount Bonnell. The western sky was lit up in all the colors of a dish of variegated candy with the "spry pinks, shy lemons, greens, coo l choc olates s" and all, and just in front of me on the International & Great Northern Railroad was a heavy freight "lo co mo tive s pouting vi o lets."

As striking as they are, if these unconventional, anomalous, puzzling oddities were all that Mr. Cummings had to offer, I would not be inclined to esteem him so very highly as a poet. Has he written anything that we can really call great poetry? I think he has. He has composed a number of charming and erratic child poems, a score or more of very odd and striking sonnets, eighteen or twenty amorphous but provocative portrait sketches, dozens of lovely songs, an extended Epithalamion that will bear comparison with Spenser's highly decorative efforts in the same kind, and several love poems which I think are unsurpassed in modern lyric poetry. I shall cite only two examples of his somewhat more regular and conventional verse to prove my point. And since these *are* more nearly conventional in their form, more nearly like the poetry we have been trained to respond to, we can more easily make the comparison with similar poems with which we are familiar, and thus judge whether we have here real poetry or mere verbal jugglery and cleverness.

Take first the following sonnet, much more regular in its pattern than most of Mr. Cummings' efforts in this form:

This is the garden. Time shall surely reap,
and on Death's blade may lie a flower curled,
strong silent greens serenely lingering,
absolute lights like baths of golden snow.

This is the garden: pursed lips do blow
upon cool flutes within wide glooms, and sing
(of harps celestial to the quivering string)
invisible faces hauntingly and slow.

This is the garden. Time shall surely reap,
and on Death's blade may lie a flower curled,
in other lands where other songs be sung;
yet stand They here enraptured, as among
the slow deep trees perpetual of sleep
some silver-fingered fountain steals the world.

The magic of this sonnet is evident; the poem needs no commendation to one who has an ear for music or an eye for beauty.

The second selection is a love song entitled "Of Nicolette." It is an artist's study in white, written in regular five-stressed lines arranged in an original rime pattern of eight lines, abccbdda. The sequence of the four stanzas may be outlined as follows: (1) The castle on a moonlight night in the lover's month of May; (2) Nicolette, touched by love, (3) glides forth from an open door of the castle, and (4) walks forth into the garden to meet her lover.

"Of Nicolette"

dreaming in marble all the castle lay
like some gigantic ghost-flower born of night
blossoming in white towers to the moon,
soft sighed the passionate darkness to the tune
of tiny troubadours, and (phantom-white)
dumb-blooming boughs let fall their glorious snows,
and the unearthly sweetness of a rose
swam upward from the troubled heart of May;

a Winged Passion woke and one by one
there fell upon the night, like angel's tears,
the syllables of that mysterious prayer,
and as an opening lily drowsy-fair
(when from her couch of poppy petals peers
the sleepy morning) gently draws apart
her curtains, and lays bare her trembling heart,
with beads of dew made jewels by the sun,

so one high shining tower (which as a glass
turned light to flame and blazed with snowy fire)
unfolding, gave the moon a nymphlike face,
a form whose snowy symmetry of grace
haunted the limbs as music haunts the lyre,

a creature of white hands, who letting fall
a thread of lustre from the castle wall
glided, a drop of radiance, to the grass—

shunning the sudden moonbeam's treacherous snare
she sought the harboring dark, and (catching up her
delicate silk) all white, with shining feet,
went forth into the dew: right wildly beat
her heart at every kiss of daisy-cup,
and from her cheek the beauteous color went
with every bough that reverently bent
to touch the yellow wonder of her hair.

If this is not great lyrical poetry, then I am no judge. Personally I confess that I have not been so thrilled by throbbing melody, exalted lyricism, idealized passion, beautifully imaginative imagery, and the sheer singing power of English words since in my youth I surrendered to the spell of Meredith's "Love in the Valley" and Keats' "Ode to the Nightingale."

Professor Payne's favorable review, naturally, pleased Cummings. When he received a copy he wrote Payne.

24/1/26

Dear Professor Payne:

Thanks for the copy of the "Longhorn Magazine," containing your article. I was much pleased to note that you put Painter first and poet second.

Unfortunately, I cannot suggest a vehicle for the wider circulation of this article; for the very reason that my relations with publishers and periodicals are neither extensive nor (as a rule) cordial (of which situation am far from being proud).

Have loaned your article to the staff of "Boni & Liveright," that notable disorganization which plans to emit my next book—a copy of which book will, I trust, reach you at the proper time—with the hope that your "views" may "do some good" there.

Very frankly, what most pleases me about your enthusiasm for my efforts is: the feeling, which I have, that you yourself are greatly enjoying the exploration of "modern art" in general and "modern painting" in particular. The as-it-were candle infinitely being worth the (so to speak) game, I trust this will continue—

Yours,
e. e. cummings

4 Patchin Place
New York

CHAPTER SIX

Of Edwin Arlington Robinson

W(H)EN Professor Payne's passion for Cummings' poetry passed at the end of the 1920s, he believed Edwin Arlington Robinson "the profoundest and therefore greatest, of our living American poets. . . ." Payne predicted that Robinson's best poems would last "for centuries" and "be read by generations unborn."

Professor Payne and Robinson resembled each other physically; they stood tall and lanky. They were both humble, modest men, refusing self-advertisement. Robinson shied from publicity and when he finally became famous, rather late in life, he refused to go after money on the lecture circuit. Dr. Payne gave selflessly to both students and famous writers, and took no credit for the successes of either. Both men valued decency highly. Robinson answered Dr. Payne's letters immediately like a gentleman. He never left Dr. Payne waiting months or a year for an answer as did Robert Frost.

Professor Payne saw a dark and depressing tone in much of Robinson's poetry but said that Robinson's tragic figures were often lighted up with humor and a sense of hope.

Dr. Payne noted with pleasure that Robinson's final verdict on life spoke of some far-off divine event toward which the soul of man moves. Both Professor Payne and Robinson believed that life is hard and that life's hardness could be tempered through faith, and the pursuit of poetry could help sustain that faith in troubled times.

Professor Payne believed *The Man Against the Sky*, published in 1916, represented Robinson's best volume of poetry. The vision in *The Man Against the Sky* portrays life as horrible, therefore it must have meaning.[1] How did Robinson come to see life as horrible? How did Robinson develop the hypothesis that mankind actually lived in hell and did not know it?[2]

A child does not have to be a genius to feel if his arrival in his family is desired. Robinson *was* a genius and immediately and instinctively understood that he was not what the family "ordered" when he was born on December 22, 1869.

Robinson's mother had hoped for a baby girl after two sons. Robinson's mother considered his birth "unwelcome and disturbing." She felt a girl should have been born so she could be to her what her two boys were to their father. Mary Robinson, his mother, believed that a girl had been withheld from her. Incredibly the family did not even bother to give the baby a name. The family did not get around to naming the baby until the summer of 1870 and they did it in a cavalier manner that can only be called shocking. They drew lots! A lady from Arlington, Massachusetts drew the name Edwin from a hat. In her honor, the family gave him Arlington for a middle name.[3] No wonder Robinson believed in fate. But fate in Robinson's life did not stop there.

Robinson once spent nine dreary months as a time-checker during construction of the first New York subway. Then he became unemployed again. The intervention of none other than the President of the United States secured Robinson work in the Government Customs House on Wall Street in New York in June, 1905.

President Theodore Roosevelt's son Kermit had read Robinson's *The Children of the Night* while studying at Choate, the elite eastern prep school that would later educate John F. Kennedy. Robinson's work so impressed Kermit he sent a copy of *The Children of the Night* to his father, an unusual man of letters among U.S. presidents. Teddy Roosevelt was equally impressed with the volume of poetry which had been published by Robinson himself in 1897 as a gift to his mother. Who would not be? *The Children of the Night* included those two powerful poems, "Richard Corey" and "Miniver Cheevey."

President Roosevelt not only secured Robinson the Customs House job but actively intervened on Robinson's behalf in the literary world, himself writing a review of *The Children of the Night* for *The Outlook* magazine and convincing *Scribner's* magazine to publish Robinson. *Scribner's* published twelve Robinson poems between 1906 and 1910.[4] Robinson was not yet a national sensation, but he had made a breakthrough.

How President Roosevelt had learned of Robinson's need of a job is unclear, but what is clear is that Robinson's breakthrough provided financial security only briefly, for Teddy Roosevelt lost both the Republican nomination and a third party bid for the presidency in 1908. The election of William Howard Taft naturally provided a housecleaning of political appointees. Yet Taft aide William Loeb, father of the infamous publisher, had been the Roosevelt aide who had placed Robinson in the Customs House in the first place. Left to his own desires, Loeb might not have dismissed Robinson. But too many Customs House workers complained that if they were being dismissed, so too should the poet, who did no Customs House work. Robinson, like Hawthorne, had been given a government job so he would have time to write, not do government work. But bending to the inhouse outcry, Loeb dismissed Robinson.

Once again out of work, Robinson borrowed and lived with friends to survive. From 1911 on, Robinson lived for free at the Peterborough artist colony in New Hampshire during the summer. Not until 1922 did Robinson live entirely by his writing, and not until 1926 with the unexpected 57,475 sales of *Tristram* did Robinson become financially secure.[5]

Dr. Payne did for Robinson what he did for Young, Dobie, Masters, Sandburg, and Robert Frost; he reviewed his poems, collected his works, and when he had a question regarding the poet's meaning, he sat down and wrote Robinson a letter.

Robinson's first Pulitzer Prize came in 1921 for his *Collected Poems* and his second in 1924 for *The Man Who Died Twice*. Robinson's *Tristram*, so popular, won Robinson a third Pulitzer Prize in 1927 and was his third volume of poetry based on the King Arthur legend. The first two were *Merlin* (1917), and *Lancelot* (1920). Payne wanted to know Robinson's sources for the poems. Robinson said Payne's students would not have a great amount of research to find his sources. Robinson said he used the traditional outlines in Malory and the French story of Tristram. Robinson said he used a variant of Malory's ending for his *Tristram*, but he said that he mostly made up his Arthurian poems. Robinson told

Payne the three volumes of poetry based on the King Arthur legends should be read merely as romantic poems founded on familiar legends.

When Robinson's *Matthias At The Door* was published in 1931, Professor Payne reviewed it with enthusiasm for *The Dallas Morning News*.

"Matthias At The Door"
by L. W. Payne, Jr.

The appearance of a new poem by Edwin Arlington Robinson may be said to mean to the poetry readers of the present time what the announcement of a new play by Shakespeare must have meant to the habitual theater attendants of Elizabethan times. We watch for the announcement of a Robinson poem, scoop it up from the counters of the bookstores, and hie away to a quiet corner to plunge into its mysterious depths with the same sort of eagerness, expectancy, and enthusiasm that the Elizabethan playgoers must have experienced when an "Othello," a "King Lear," or a "Hamlet" was announced for its initial performance at the Old Globe Theater.

This new poem, "Matthias at the Door," falls into the category of those psychological studies of modern life which Robinson has been giving us steadily since he completed, with "Tristram" (1927), his adventure into the domain of medieval romance. "Matthias" (pronounced ma-thigh' as, Mr. Robinson desires us to remember) is in the same vein as "Cavender's House" (1929) and "The Glory of the Nightingales" (1930), displaying the same kind of psychological analysis, using some of the same technical devices, portraying somewhat similar characters, and interpreting similar problems in the complex modern social system. For example, Cavender's long conversation with the spirit of Laramie, the wife whom he had murdered twelve years before the story opens, there in his now deserted home is exactly paralleled in the opening section of "Matthias" when the protagonist visits that "wood shadowed and forsaken gorge" filled with "monstrous and unreal rocks," a fearsome place where a year before his friend Garth had committed suicide and hidden himself in a dark hole behind a strange door in the face of a huge rock shaped like an Egyptian tomb. In each case the disturbed conscience of the main character causes the character to create out of his own subconscious ego the spirit of the dead person, and hold long searching and coherent conversations with the departed, supplying the words, the speech tones, and the gestures of the dead person out of his own diseased and distorted imagination. And similarly, the study of the character of the rich, willfully egotistic, and apparently successful Nightingale is duplicated in the study of the hard, self-satisfied, and apparently successful Matthias, particularly in their blind, consuming egotism and pride and in the final conversion or transformation of each of them at the end of the poem—though Nightingale finds his solution by removing himself from the scene in order to leave his wealth immediately available for the service of mankind through the amelioration of the ravages of disease, while Matthias finds his by living instead of dying, returning, at Garth's suggestion, from the dark door and being born to a new life to be devoted to the construction of a worthy tower of sympathy toward and service to mankind.

The story is clearer, more direct, easier, to read at first trial than is usually the case in the Robinsonian narrative. The opening conversation between Garth's ghost and Matthias is at first a little puzzling, since it does not immediately appear that Garth is not a real live man but merely a figment of Matthias' brain; a second reading of Part I, after the situation has been cleared up in later sections, will reveal numerous hints which ought to have led one to divine immediately the true situation.

Not quite so dramatic as "Cavender's House" nor quite so melodramatic as "The Glory of the Nightingales," "Matthias" is much more stimulating and profound in its ethical and psychological import than either of its immediate predecessors. The conversion or complete transformation of a human soul has an ethical import far beyond that displayed in the confession of a guilty conscience, as in the case of Cavender, or a sort of premortuary transformation as in the case of the Nightingale. Matthias is not alive, for he has never been born:

> *"It seems a mystery that so many should live*
> *Who are not born, but that's the infinite way."*

Robinson suggests, but he does not use, the familiar phrase of the New Testament, "Ye must be born again." In fact, Matthias was an orthodox religious person, one who clung to and thought he found much solace in his faith, and there is a touch of irony in making him deny God and renounce his faith before he can be really born.

It is through suffering, both his own and that of his friends, that he is eventually born.

For the presentation of such abstruce subject matter, such subtle philosophic and ethical ideas as this poem contains, Robinson has perfected through infinite patience and long discipline a style of remarkable resilience, ductility, and flexibility. That is to say, he displays economy, fluency, and variety as the need of the case demands. The directness of the flow of his language is remarkable; so far as I have noted there is not an inverted expression in the whole poem. The blank verse flows along so smoothly and steadily, always in the calm, elevated tone of philosophic speech, that one forgets he is reading verse but never that he is immersed in poetry. The body, the form, the words, the meter of the poem are well nigh perfect in their adaptability to the theme, as we have learned to expect these things to be if Robinson's name is signed to the poem; but there is more than mere excellence of form and style. The very essence of poetry—the creative imagination, the probing insight into mysteries, the paradox of saying in words what cannot be said, in other words the high classic quality of restrained and balanced suggestiveness—all this makes "Matthias at the Door" one more spacious and lovely room in Robinson's ever-expanding palace of art.

One does not expect much of the purely lyrical and decorative types of poetic ornament in a narrative poem, but "Matthias" is by no means devoid of passages of sheer beauty, nor of those subtle symbolic images and allusions that spring the imagination. For example, in the opening description of the wild, rocky gorge where the Egyptian-like rock tomb, itself a symbol of death, located in sight of Matthias' elegant home, and to the dark door of which all four characters are successfully drawn, the note of hope is struck by a reference to the trees, which

"To a straightness and height
That would not elsewhere have been theirs thrust up
Their tops to find the sun;"

and to the brook, which down there "somewhere unseen made a cold song of eternity." And throughout the poem the references are from time to time repeated, "the trees lifting their heads to the sky" and "the cold, shadow-hidden brook down there" singing its note of hope. Even at the very end of the poem Matthias suddenly heard

"A tinkling in the night like a small music
That had been always and would always be,
And was a brook."

Aphoristic and epigrammatic lines are naturally more to be expected, and Robinson, as usual, supplies a number of quotable passages in this new poem. To give the poet the last word I quote a few of these:

"Accomplishment and honor are not the same,
Matthias; and one may live without the other."

"Half the grief
Of living is our not seeing what's not to be
Before we see too well."

Pity is like a knife,
Sometimes, and it may pierce one who employs it
More shrewdly than the victim it would save."

"We are prisoners now and pupils in a school
Where often our best rewards appear to us
To be our punishments."

A year later Robinson's book of eleven poems, *Nicodemus,* appeared. The thirteen-page poem "Nicodemus," from which the volume's title was taken, was written at great inspiration in three days.[6]

In Dr. Payne's review for *The Dallas Morning News* in October, 1932, he devoted a good deal of space to the volume's last poem, "The March of the Cameron Men." "The March of the Cameron Men," wrote Payne, is a subtle and somewhat mystifying study of a love scene between a doctor and a young widow whose husband the two of them have practically murdered, that is, they have tacitly allowed the husband to die when the doctor's skill might have saved him. Payne said the crucial third stanza of the poem subtly suggests disaster to the proposed union of the guilty lovers. Responding to Professor Payne's remarks, Robinson said Dr. Payne read more into the poem than Robinson had in mind. Robinson said that he meant the reader to infer that the woman in the poem had no intention of marrying the doctor after he had done his dirty work. Robinson also said that in the third stanza of the poem the doctor was half revealing his own doubts about marrying the woman. Robinson added that the poem is intended to be psychological, just a little obscure.

Dr. Payne was less enthusiastic about Robinson's last volume of poetry, *Amaranth*. Written in a hurry during the summer of 1933, *Amaranth* was published in 1934 and critics roundly rebuffed it.[7] Dr. Payne responded to the poetry more warmly than most critics but thought Robinson's character creation was below his usual efforts. Professor Payne wrote to Robinson on Christmas Day, 1934. What follows is taken from Dr. Payne's own carbon copy of the letter.

University of Texas
December 25, 1934

Dear Mr. Robinson:

I have been in close communion with you these first two days of my Christmas vacation. The truth is that I made a faint stab at *Amaranth* when it appeared in our bookstores here in October. I think it was, but I didn't get as much out of the first efforts as I usually do from my first perusal of your new poems. I was engaged in an additional job of my own all during the fall season, and so I could not bring my full faculties to bear control of my temporal program so as to give myself sufficient uninterrupted hours to read with any real satisfaction a real allegory like this one. I began two days before Christmas and read *Amaranth* through three times successfully before the 25th, and I think I now have the argument well in control. I really enjoyed this concentrated and consecutive reading—the only sort of reading that will suffice for such a poem. I rather suspect and fear, however, that this last work of yours will find fewer admirers than anything you have written in recent years—not because it does not deserve admirers, but because it will find few readers who are tough enough to give it the necessary gray matter and stand up under the necessary mental drubbing which the allegory demands.

Most of all I enjoyed the mild irony and dry humor of the poems. There is a lot of truth back of the main thesis, of the poem, mainly that there are many misfits and incongruities in this mortal life of ours; and there are few of us who have the nerve of a Fargo to see,

Amaranth, that is, our own limitations and give up our impossible ambitions to be or make of ourselves what we are not natively capable of being or making of ourselves. I enjoyed particularly Pink the poet's lecture to the various misfits in Part II, and I almost laughed aloud with satisfaction at the attack on the modern school of artists who go in for unintelligibility, as in the case of Atlas, the painter who was drunk on color and made a blue horse with never a line in it anywhere to tell one that it was a horse. The names of the characters are admirably chosen too—Amaranth, Fargo, Figg, Styx, Flax, Ipswich, Ampersand, Watchman. To me they never become real persons, but that is as it should be in an allegory like this. For philosophic criticism of life and art you have never done better, but for character creation you have always done better in your more realistic narratives than you have in this abstraction, *me judice*. It is well enough to take a fling like this to satisfy yourself that you can do this sort of thing, but I hope you will get back to real men and women in your next lest you alienate a large portion of your readers. I am very doubtful whether I can interest my college students in *Amaranth*, for example, as I interested them two years ago in *Matthias at the Door*. What young readers want is dramatic action, the existing force of a human problem, and they resent the substitution of typical puppets for real flesh-and-blood creations. But this is not a preachment to divest you from the path that your genius leads you to follow. You have done enough of the dramatic type of narrative to justify your indulgence in any other kind of composition that you care to give us. I for one am not disposed to complain for I have had a great time slowly digesting your latest excellent piece of poetry. I am thoroughly disgusted with the adverse brief criticism of *Amaranth* which I saw in the New Republic where I saw some woman's screed on *Amaranth*.

I am enclosing you a few proof readings after the manner of my former suggestions—which you rather welcomed than resented, if I interpreted you right.

When will you be giving us another revised *Collected Poems?* I think you should take care to give the world your final reunions and inclusions before very much longer. Life is brittle, you know and I should like to see you finish your reunions before you take your departure hence.

L. W. PAYNE, JR.

71

But Dr. Payne was behind Robinson's schedule for "final reunions," and what Robinson thought of this last Payne letter will never be known. Robinson was very sick and could not answer. At the end of January Robinson underwent exploratory surgery which revealed widespread cancer. For the obvious reasons, doctors told Robinson he suffered from arthritis and stomach trouble.[8] Robinson died less than three months later on April 6, 1935.

We know how highly Dr. Payne regarded Robinson among American poets. What did Robinson think of Dr. Payne? The best answer to that question came in Robinson's letter to Payne on November 25, 1932. Robinson said Dr. Payne's interest in his work had always meant a great deal to him. Robinson said he may not have always expressed that appreciation adequately in his letters.

A Robinson Epilogue:

Dr. Payne took great pride in his bibliographical study "The First Edition of E. A. Robinson's 'The Peterborough Idea.'" Originally published in 1939 in The University of Texas *Studies in English*, the article was later bound in soft cover and sent to practically everyone Dr. Payne knew.

Professor Payne's bibliographical study contained an investigation into Robinson's famous essay "The Peterborough Idea," first published in the *North American Review* in September, 1916. The essay explained the purposes of the Peterborough Artist Colony, where he spent his summers, and provided an intimate look into the workings of the colony. Immediately afterwards the essay was revised by Robinson and issued as a pamphlet sometime in the late autumn of 1916, according to Dr. Payne's exhaustive research. The pamphlet had not been dated.

Dr. Payne read both the essay and pamphlet and found the revisions Robinson had made for the pamphlet. Since most sources had listed the publication of the pamphlet as 1917, Dr. Payne had made a major bibliographic discovery. Such a fact may seem trivial to a reader looking at the issue forty-seven years later, but to a literary scholar who had spent considerable time in researching the issue, it offered a source of tremendous satisfaction. Indeed,

Dr. Payne felt as proud of his thirteen-page pamphlet as almost any other bit of scholarship he had done in his entire life.

Since Edwin Arlington Robinson did not participate in the university lecture circuit, he never came to Austin and consequently never met Dr. Payne. Nevertheless Professor Payne's daughter Sarah did meet Robinson.

Sarah Payne had been graduated with honors from The University of Texas in 1930 and was studying psychology at Columbia University when Robinson extended an invitation for her to visit him.

Robinson left New York as early as possible every year to go to New Hampshire for the summer. He suggested Sarah visit him some afternoon before March 20. She accepted the invitation and called on Robinson on March 18, 1931.

Since 1922, Robinson had been living with James and Laura Fraser, first at 28 West Eighth Street in New York, and beginning in 1927, at 328 East Forty-Second Street.[9] Sarah found Robinson's place on 42nd Street hard to locate.

"As I remember," she said, "I arrived at the approximate address on time. However, there was no number—and I wandered around a little, but was worried about being late. I decided to ring the doorbell at this place and he opened the door himself. He was delighted to see me, for he realized from my note that I had the wrong number. From the entrance we went up some stairs and there was a party in the drawing room. I caught a glimpse of what I now know was a cocktail party, but he gestured toward them and said we would go up to his study. It was a charming room with lots of books.

"I knew that it was a great privilege to visit with the great poet, but I really did it to please my father. I had written a term paper on his poem *Tristram*, so I felt at ease with him.

"Mr. Robinson said he would have liked to meet my father but seemed pleased to entertain me. I told him about Dad and his devotion to his students and his joy in literature. Actually Robinson was physically much like my father. He quizzed me about my studies and asked me 'what is this psychology?'

73

"Psychology is an attempt to understand the human mind," I replied.

"'That's impossible!' he said."

CHAPTER SEVEN

Promoter and Critic

PROFESSOR Payne supplemented his income in the 1920s and 1930s by writing reviews for *The Dallas Morning News* and the *Sherman Daily Democrat*, Sherman, Texas; and by writing anthologies—a subject explored in chapter ten. Dr. Payne contributed in 1920 to *Kind Words,* a young people's weekly published by the Southern Baptist Publication Board of Nashville. Dr. Payne also wrote a series of articles called "Fifty Famous Southern Poets," for approximately six Southern newspapers, including *The Charlotte Observer,* which used these poems and notes as syndicated Sunday issue features. Each of the fifty poems reproduced carried a short introductory critical and historical note.

Dr. Payne and his friend A. J. Armstrong of Baylor University, a fellow folklorist and curator of Baylor's impressive Browning Collection, also acted as promoters of literary greats. The two Texans played host to famous writers in Waco and Austin and arranged their speaking engagements throughout Texas.

One of Professor Payne's first promotions occurred during World War I, when he served as chairman of the University lecture committee. In that capacity, Dr. Payne introduced British poet John Masefield in March, 1918. Masefield spoke on war conditions in Europe at University Methodist Church in Austin.

Armstrong, the long-time chairman of Baylor's English Department, 1912–1952, wrote Dr. Payne on March 8, 1919, to say that Vachel Lindsay would agree to lecture at Baylor and Texas if they would pay him $137.50 for each engagement. Armstrong said Lindsay was especially interested in The University of Texas. The two folklorists brought the great Irish poet, William Butler Yeats, to Texas in 1920. Dr. Payne met but did not get an opportunity to speak with Yeats during the poet's Austin visit.

When Armstrong wrote from Waco on March 28, 1925, announcing that he had secured fifteen engagements for the great poet Harriet Monroe, Dr. Payne was hearing about an old friend. Dr. Payne had first visited Monroe in Chicago in 1919. They met again in Chicago in 1923. Armstrong said Monroe agreed to speak for $100 per engagement, had two open dates, and would be willing to fill those times by speaking for only $50. Since everyone else was paying $100, including Baylor, Armstrong urged Professor Payne not to reveal the fact that The University of Texas could get her to speak for $50. Armstrong reported that Monroe had spoken at Baylor several years before and was "highly satisfactory." Dr. Payne's arm did not have to be twisted and Harriet Monroe lectured at The University of Texas for the first time in April, 1925.

Having been given the honor of introducing Monroe in Austin, Dr. Payne said that Alice Corbin Henderson, traveling with Monroe, was one of the founders of *Poetry* magazine. Monroe held her tongue on the matter while in Austin, but when she stopped later at the Washington Hotel in Shreveport, Louisiana, for rest, she wrote Dr. Payne to say she alone founded *Poetry* and that later she had hired Henderson as an associate editor.

Despite the question of Henderson's role in *Poetry*, Monroe said she had a wonderful time in Austin and said she appreciated the kindnesses shown her by the Paynes. She said she would think of them in the hills under the pink dome of the Capitol.

Professors Payne and Armstrong brought another writer, Edna St. Vincent Millay, to Texas. Miss Millay appeared in a reading at Hogg Memorial Auditorium on The University of Texas campus on November 16, 1934.

Dr. Payne and his daughter Sarah sat in the second row left of stage. Sarah happened to be in Austin on a visit; she had married Jack Foxworth of Dallas in 1932. Miss Millay began her performance by reading a number of earlier poems including "The Buck in the Snow" and "The Ballad of the Harp-weaver." She then read from her one-act play "Departure." After reading sonnets from *Fatal Interview*, Millay turned to her new book, *Wine from those Grapes*, just a few weeks off the press. She concluded her program with three short poems portraying child life and thought. On being recalled to the stage she read as an encore one of her earlier favorites, "Travel." Dr. Payne said Millay had been received by perhaps 700 persons, a good crowd in Hogg Auditorium. Professor Payne remarked that Miss Millay was a "dramatic, not a natural, reader; but one must admit that she is a great dramatic reader." Afterwards Professor Payne and Sarah went back stage and chatted with Millay.

As has been previously suggested, Professor Payne was not a passive critic. He challenged authors, writing letters to question interpretations, ask for clarifications, offer his own opinions. In 1928 Dr. Payne wrote poet Wallace Stevens with questions and interpretations of six of Stevens' poems. The six poems were: "Peter Quince at the Clavier," "Sunday Morning," "Le Monocle de Mon Oncle," "Thirteen Ways of Looking at a Blackbird," "Domination of Black," and "To the One of Fictive Music."

Wallace Stevens replied to Professor Payne in a candid letter, so candid Stevens ordered Payne to destroy the letter. Payne, however, saved the letter and it was originally published by Alfred A. Knopf in *Letters of Wallace Stevens*, 1966. The letter is reprinted here with permission from Knopf and Stevens' daughter, Holly Stevens.

690 Asylum Avenue
Hartford, Conn., March 31, 1928

L. W. Payne, Jr.,
2104 Pearl Street
Austin, Texas

Dear Sir:
I am surprised to find that some weeks have already passed since you wrote me.

It is very difficult for me to change things from one category to another, and, as a matter of fact, I dislike to do so. It may or may not be like converting a piece of logic. But the feeling is much the same. I shall return your notes and I shall dictate briefly a comment or two.

77

Peter Quince: Your understanding of this is quite right. Somebody once called my attention to the fact that there were no Byzantines in Susanna's time. I hope that that bit of precious pedantry will seem as unimportant to you as it does to me.

Sunday Morning: This is not essentially a woman's meditation on religion and the meaning of life. It is anybody's meditation. To judge from your comment on II, you are taking the thing a little too literally. The poem is simply an expression of paganism, although of course, I did not think that I was expressing paganism when I wrote it.

Of the last two lines, it is probably the last that is obscure to you. Life is as fugitive as dew upon the feet of men dancing in dew. Men do not either come from any direction or disappear in any direction. Life is as meaningless as dew.

Now these ideas are not bad in a poem. But they are a frightful bore when converted as above.

Le Monocle de Mon Oncle: That means of course My Uncle's Monocle, or merely a certain point of view. Certainly the choice of words is intentional, although these words are not an instance of clashed edges. In addition to the excitement of suave sounds, there is an excitement, an insistent provocation in the strange cacophonies of words.

I am not dictating this from a copy of the book. My recollection is that the Mother of Heaven was merely somebody to swear by, and that the reference was not symbolic.

Your analysis of this poem is much too close. I am sure that I never had in mind the many abstractions that appear in your analysis. I had in mind simply a man fairly well along in life, looking back and talking in a more or less personal way about life.

I am sorry that I am not able to tell you offhand just what the meaning of "the much crumpled thing" is, [line 16] because, I do not recall the line. The reading of the proofs of the book gave me such a horror of it that I have hardly looked at it since it was published, and I don't think that the "thing" was sex appeal. I am some hundreds of years behind other people, and it is going to be a long time before I let a commercialism like sex appeal get any farther from the front fence.

It may seem inconsistent after that to explain the lines "Why without pity" [line 32] etc. as meaning simply that the speaker was speaking to a woman whose hair was still down.

I cannot say your comments on each of the other parts of this poem are right. But I notice at the foot of page 3 your remark: "Old age is a rose rabbi pursuing the philosophic ideal." Not at all. One is a rose rabbi and pursues a philosophic ideal of life when one is young. ["But the text proves him wrong here," Payne scribbled in the margin.]

Thirteen Ways: As to VII: "In Haddam, Connecticut, men grow thin seeking gold," do please leave out that Connecticut. I am told that men did dig gold in Haddam, Connecticut, once, but that seems like rubbing it in.

This group of poems is not meant to be a collection of epigrams or of ideas, but of sensations.

The Domination of Black: I am sorry that a poem of this sort has to contain any ideas at all, because its sole purpose is to fill the mind with the images and sounds that it contains. A mind that examines such a poem for its prose contents gets absolutely nothing from it. You are supposed to get heavens full of the colors and full of sounds, and you are supposed to feel as you would feel if you actually got all this.

To The One of Fictive Music: This poem was rather more thought out than the last one. It is not only children who live in a world of imagination. All of us do that. But after living there to the degree that a poet does, the desire to get back to the everyday world becomes so keen that one turns away from the imaginative world in a most definite and determined way. Another way of putting it is that, after writing a poem, it is a good thing to walk around the block; after too much midnight, it is pleasant to hear the milkman, and yet, and this is the point of the poem, the imaginative world is the only real world, after all.

It is shocking to have to say this sort of thing. Please destroy these notes. I don't mind your seeing what I have said here. But I don't want you to quote me. No more explanations.

Yours very truly,
WALLACE STEVENS

Dr. Payne, as noted elsewhere, often wrote reviews of his friends' books. The following review of an American history text by his fishing partner Eugene Barker and another UT colleague Walter Webb appeared in the December, 1928 issue of *The Texas*

Outlook. It should be mentioned that Professor Payne had edited and proofread the book before its publication.

"New Viewpoints in History of American Life"
Reviewed by Dr. L. W. Payne, University of Texas

The Growth of a Nation by Professors Eugene C. Barker and Walter P. Webb of The University of Texas and William E. Dodd of the University of Chicago is certainly the most beautiful and attractive and probably, both from the standpoints of matter included and of pedagogic arrangement, the most satisfactory textbook on United States history that has yet been made. All three of the authors are successful teachers and research scholars and authorities in American history, and they have been bold enough to advance new ideas, materials, and methods in the presentation of American history in school book form. There was a time when most of the history in our school books was an elaboration of wars and military achievements with a small amount of political history interlarded. The new ideal of history is to present the whole life of a people in such a way as to make the student realize just what the people were doing from period to period. It includes the industrial, the economic, the social, and the cultural life as well as the military history. In fact, the military history is now properly subordinated to its true proportion and value in the whole life of the nation.

A nation, like an individual, has its ancestors, its predecessors, its forebears. In studying the life story of an individual we first want to know something about his antecedents, his family, his ancestral inheritance as it were. So the authors of this new and striking story of the life growth of civilization from the dawn of history in ancient Egypt and Babylonia trace in rapid flight the important events of world history up to the time when men were seeking a new route to the East Indies—the time when Columbus wanted to test the then new theory of the roundness of the earth by sailing westward instead of eastward to reach the far-famed Indies. This survey is presented in simple and graphic style, and the whole story from one end of the book to the other holds the interest almost as does a romantic tale. Colored maps and pictures, diagrams and drawings in rich abundance help to make every chapter both clear and attractive to the young reader.

We are rather proud of the fact that the names of two distinguished Texans fly at the headmast of this new ship on the sea of historical literature. In this book, for the first time perhaps, the South and the West are given their due proportion of attention in the history of the nation. There is no sectional note, no over-emphasis on anything Southern or Western merely because it is that; but these sections as integral parts of the nation are given their due proportion of attention according to their growing importance. All sections are fused into one nation, and each one is accorded adequate and judicious treatment. There can be no cavil or contest raised on this point either by pupils and patrons or scholars. We are proud of the fact that such a book has come out of Texas and Chicago.

We confidently predict that this valuable new contribution to the school histories of America will lead all competitors until other historians shall pay *The Growth of a Nation* the high compliment of imitation, both of its style and method and of its matter and judicious proportion, and thus produce an equally beautiful and satisfactory type of book for the children of the nation to study.

Clarence Ayres, another University of Texas colleague, wrote a fascinating biography of Thomas Huxley in 1932. It was Huxley, as Payne notes in the following review, who was responsible for popularizing Darwin's theory of evolution. How the devout Baptist Payne looked at the biography of the popularizer of evolution provides interesting reading.

"New Book on Thomas Huxley by Professor Clarence Ayres"
Reviewed by L. W. Payne, Jr.

The principal point upon which Professor Ayres predicates a re-evaluation of Thomas Huxley's contribution to the advancement of knowledge, and hence civilization, is the fact that to Huxley rather than to Darwin is due the credit of establishing evolution as the accepted mode of creation, and of bringing the word evolution into the specific meaning which it commonly connotes in our time. Darwin was a mild, retiring, non-self-assertive type of investigative scientist, who carefully and painstakingly gathered facts on the causes of the variation in species in the animal and plant kingdoms. Huxley was a popular lecturer and debater, a propagandist, a promoter, a defender of the accredited and accomplished results of scientific investigation. Darwin may be said to have laid the egg of modern theory, but it was Huxley who incubated it and made the public aware of the deductions regarding man's place in nature which Darwin's theory of the origin of the species made inevitable. It was Darwin who proposed the idea of variation of species on the basis of natural selection, the survival of the fittest, and the gradual adaption to environment. But it was Huxley who attacked the problem from the point of view of man's place in nature on the basis of the theories, which, when Darwin first propounded them, Huxley promptly accepted as reasonable and worthy of acceptance as proven truths. The very title of Huxley's greatest book indicates this fact: "Man's Place in Nature."

Except by inference there is not one word in Darwin's "The Origin of Species" regarding man's descent from the higher form of anthropoid apes. He gathered the experimental facts and provable truths concerning the variation of species among domesticated animals and plants as directed by the will of man, and then deduced his theory of natural selection as the basis of changes in species in wild nature unassisted by the will of man. The only single passage in "The Origin of Species" which touches on the effects of Darwin's theory on man's place in the theory which he propounded occurs on the next to the last page of his conclusion to the volume; it reads as follows:

"In the distant future I see open fields for far more important researches. Psychology will be based on a new foundation, that of the necessary acquirement of each mental power and capacity by graduation. *Light will be thrown on the origin of man and his history."* (The italics are mine.)

Some years ago I acquired a copy of the first American edition of Darwin's "Origin of Species." When I examined the book, the first thing I expected to see was a picture of man as the offspring of monkeys. I looked in vain for any reference to what I had always supposed was Darwin's view, namely, that man was, in his physical form at least, the direct descendent of the higher forms of apes. I read and read and looked and looked until I became tired. Then I turned to the conclusion, and when my eye lit upon the short paragraph which I have just quoted I at once concluded that the whole book had been written with that final sentence referring to the origin of man as the ultimate objective. Certainly the long and hard-fought war over the Darwinian theory raged over that point.

Dr. Ayres clearly shows that it was Huxley and not Darwin who fought the embattled forces of conservatism and religion on this very point. Still I cannot help thinking that Dr. Ayres goes too far when he wishes to shift the responsibility and, along with the responsibility, the honor of promulgating the modern theory of evolution from Darwin's to Huxley's shoulders. Both deserve praise, the one for initiating the theory, the other for fighting the battles which led to its general acceptance. It goes without saying, however, that Darwinism will never be supplanted by Huxleyism as the popular generic name for the theory.

CHAPTER EIGHT

Frost's Friend

THE writer of Payne's generation whom he learned to admire the most and with whom he developed a strong friendship was Robert Frost. Born in 1875 in San Francisco, Frost was two years younger than Dr. Payne. Robert Lee Frost was named after the great Confederate general and one might suppose that the poet and the Alabama-born Payne shared a certain "Southern" affinity. Nothing could be further from the truth. Frost, who moved to rural Massachusetts as a youth, personified the life and ways of New England. And he always considered Ulysses S. Grant a superior military commander to Robert E. Lee.

Mutual love of poetry acted to cement the friendship of Robert Frost and L. W. Payne, Jr. Frost visited Dr. Payne several times in Austin, and they talked late into the night and well into the next day on those occasions, an excited brook of conversation babbling from these two men born in the third quarter of the nineteenth century, flung almost like aliens into the technical acrobatics of American life and literature in the twentieth century.

During these visits Professor Payne met a man far different from himself: emotionally distant from his wife, irritable, incredibly creative. For the emotionally stable Payne, the good bourgeois husband, who was gentle and kind to all, the meetings with Frost provided an opportunity to examine closely the personality of a poet. Dr. Payne wasted no minutes in Frost's presence; he maintained a laundry list of questions about Frost's poetry, the better to illuminate Frost's poetry, the better to explain the poetry to his students.

E. E. Cummings had been Dr. Payne's favorite in the 1920s, Edwin Arlington Robinson his favorite in the 1930s. But by the end of the 1930s Payne had formed the poetic judgment he would die with: Robert Frost was America's best poet. It is interesting that in 1985, forty years after Dr. Payne's death, the consensus of the American public, although not the critics, is that Robert Frost is the greatest American poet. Indeed, Robert Frost must be considered to be our national poet. Dr. Payne would be pleased by this, because he was proven right, and because he believed poetry belonged to the public, not the critics.

As far as is known, Frost always behaved pleasantly with Dr. Payne and exhibited none of his temper said to irritate others who knew him. It is therefore ironic that the most recorded and famous incident of their long friendship involved a misdated letter which gave later researchers the impression that Frost was furious with Dr. Payne.

Robert Frost first visited Dr. Payne in Austin in 1922. During that visit, they saw the Alamo in San Antonio and the San Jacinto battlefield. Frost lectured in Texas that spring, speaking in Fort Worth, Dallas, Waco, Temple, and Austin. He traveled the tour by train and complained that the trains ran always six hours late, probably an exaggeration.

Dr. Payne helped organize and promote Frost's Texas tours. One such tour occurred in 1933. Part of the tour brought Frost's return to Austin, where he had not been since the 1922 visit.

In preparation for Frost's return to Austin, Professor Payne worked frantically to ensure that Frost's visit would be a success. Professor and Mrs. Payne arranged Frost's schedule in such a way that he would be burdened only with small parties at meal times, allowing Frost as much rest and quiet as he wished. Austinites showered Dr. Payne with social requests with Frost as the honored guest. Dr. Payne limited the engagements because, as he wrote Frost, "I know you will not want to be bandied about too much."

When Frost arrived in Austin by train on Monday afternoon, April 24, 1933, he carried his exhausted body, which had delivered a lecture almost every day since he had set foot in the Lone Star State, to the white house at 2104 Pearl Street and threw himself on the hospitality of Mrs. Payne, who always catered to every need of the famous poet.

Arrangements called for Frost to speak in Hogg Memorial Auditorium on The University of Texas campus. The auditorium, not yet completed, was to have been opened for his lecture through the courtesy of the contractor, J. A. McCurdy. There would be no stage drapes or curtains adorning the 1325 seat auditorium. Frost did not speak in Hogg Auditorium. Instead Frost spoke at University Baptist Church, presumably with Payne arranging the change since he was a founding deacon of the church. Architect R. L. White insisted on the change in sites because all lighting and electrical fixtures could not be completed in time in Hogg Auditorium, and White said temporary installations in Hogg Auditorium would have been unsafe.

The Robert Frost who looked out at an audience of approximately 1,000 persons crowded into a parish designed to seat 800 persons, looked young for his fifty-eight years. His great hoard of thick grey hair hung across his forehead; his face appeared soft and youngish. He possessed a sharply pointing hawk nose, and a reporter observed him as having a "smilingly terse mouth."

Introducing Frost, Dr. H. T. Parlin, Dean of the College of Arts and Sciences, said, "He has produced a body of poetry that will live as long as any of us care to prophesy."

Speaking in a low, cracking voice, Frost brought greetings from Amherst College, where he taught, to The University of Texas. Then he began. "A poem is a picture of what we do in life," said the poet whose deep sympathy for the hard life of New England moved the hearts of Kremlin chiefs. A poet's personal life is a tough grind, Frost said. "The punishment, socially, is hard. Punishment comes from one's family, neighbors, friends, relatives, even from poetry itself."

An observer wrote that Frost spoke "in a clear, rather abrupt manner. His outflow of talk was fed by a ceaseless inflow of observation, musing, browsing, comparison-making." In this confident manner Frost launched into a reading of "Stopping by Woods on a Snowy Evening," "Mending Wall," and "Birches."

Probably his most famous poem, "Stopping by Woods on a Snowy Evening," illustrates a central human experience, the enchantment that invites listeners and readers to surrender themselves to oblivion. "Mending Wall," Frost's favorite among his own poems, captures the impulse of people to fence themselves in, to form relationships that create exclusions. "Birches" shows Frost's sense that his own personal and poetic salvation lay in facing up to the full cost, in poetry, and in daily living. Birch trees will only bear so much climbing before returning an individual, under the pressure of human weight, back home.

The poems Frost read drew portraits of country folk in a lyric way that he mingled with a philosophic narrative. He captured the actual speech tones of those of whom he wrote. He subordinated humor to character, although he revealed a mischievous vein. Frost was a realist who possessed the magic touch of strong emotion but he wrote of actuality not sentimentality. "A complete poem," he once said, "is one where an emotion has found its thought and the thought has found its word."

During the reading, Frost dramatized two of his short plays. "Death of the Hired Man" shows marital differences of taste and feeling through inadequate sensitivity of one person toward another. "The Fear" tells the story of a woman's effort to validate the imaginations that haunt a home and deprive it of its ascribed function as a place to live and love. In the plays he imitated the characters and gave impersonations of them by rising inflections in his voice and exhibiting "the way we talk up there." After Frost's reading he attended a reception given in his honor at the Faculty Men's Club.

Mrs. Frost did not start out with her husband on the lecture tour, but did meet him for the Austin visit, which came about halfway through the tour. She found him near exhaustion. When the Frosts returned north, the sensitive and tired Frost went to bed with a bad cold and stayed there for more than a week. Yet the Austin experience made a favorable impression for the Frosts. Elinor Frost wrote Mrs. Payne from Amherst to say thank you for all the hospitality. Frost, Elinor said, thought April in Texas was exactly like the middle of the summer in New England. She said Frost had noticed that the bluebonnet had just passed its prime in Texas, and that he had been impressed by the great stretches of yellow primroses he had seen. Elinor said they felt inclined to try to winter in Texas. The Frosts spent several winters in the following years in San Antonio, staying at the Menger Hotel. Bedridden with colds a good deal of the time during his San Antonio winters, Frost complained that the sun should shine in Texas more in the winter than it did.

In March of 1937, the tough old poet journeyed to Austin to lecture for a last time at The University of Texas. After arriving at 2104 Pearl Street, Frost took a nap in the guest bedroom located above the living room and that contained a nice fireplace. After his nap, he ate a light meal of poached eggs, milk and some weak tea for his nervous stomach.

When Frost left Austin he had seen Payne for the last time. Their relationships would continue by letter until Payne's death, but they would never meet again. Frost spent later winters in Florida, where presumably he saw more of the sun; but he said Florida was not as interesting as Texas.

Forty-one years after his death, Dr. Payne is remembered on the national literary scene as the man who sent a list of suggested corrections to Robert Frost concerning Frost's 1930 *Collected Poems.* The episode is filled with errors compounded by Payne himself.

Frost biographer Lawrance Thompson published a Frost letter to Payne in the *Selected Letters of Robert Frost,* 1964,[1] in which Frost tells Payne, "But you know I indulge a sort of indifference to punctuation." Thompson contended this exchange of letters caused bad blood between the two men.[2] Yet, their friendship survived. Thompson also stated that Payne served as Chairman of the English Department in The University of Texas, which is not true.

Elaine Barry in *Robert Frost on Writing,* 1973,[3] perhaps reading from Thompson's book, declared "Frost's reply reveals his barely-restrained annoyance at such misguided, if well-meant, intervention. . . ." Barry also stated that Payne was Chairman of the English Department at Texas.

More recently, Donald Hall took up the issue in the March, 1982 *Atlantic Monthly.* In his article "Robert Frost Corrupted," Hall attacked Frost editor Edward Lathem for making revisions in Frost's works. Hall contended Frost did not need revision, had no intention of making changes in his works, and cited the letter to Dr. Payne as proof that Frost refused changes in his poetry. Hall quoted Lathem as saying the Frost letter to Payne was "disarming," and then Hall declared, "But the whole letter is not so disarming as enraged" and "if I had received this letter, I would not have characterized it as disarming."[4] While Hall is probably right that Frost did not care to be corrected, he is wrong about Frost's feelings in his letter to Payne.

Unfortunately Thompson had the wrong Frost letter replying to Dr. Payne's 1930 corrections. And Dr. Payne aided Thompson's error by misdating one of his own letters.

In fairness to Thompson, he did question the date of the Frost letter. Since Payne *had* sent a list of corrections on October 19, 1930, Thompson assumed the Frost reply came soon after and labeled the date of the Frost letter as "circa November 1930" in his book. Most importantly, the issues Frost addressed in his letter had nothing to do with Dr. Payne's October 19, 1930 letter. Thompson, Barry and Hall might have drawn a different conclusion had they read both letters.

Frost's letter, so often cited, did not reply to Payne's suggested corrections of *Collected Poems* of 1930.

Frost *did* reply to Payne's suggested corrections on October 27, 1930 in a letter that apparently has never been published. The tone of Frost's letter reads much differently from the one Thompson, Barry, Lathem, and Hall have cited.

Parts of Dr. Payne's letter with the specific "corrections" that Frost replied to follow:

> The University of Texas
> Austin
> Oct. 19, 1930

Dear Robert Frost:

I have spent the whole blessed Sunday religiously reading your *Collected Poems*. My signed copy came in Saturday, and I am delighted with the book. I feel sure your "works" will go floating on down the library stream for ages to come—I might say it is *light* enough to float, but—"I'd rather he'd said it for himself." No; it is not light. It is not heavy either. It is just right to spring the mind off on a thousand journeys toward eternities. Really I feel as if I'd heard your voice all day intoning the New England drawl and putting in those stresses and italics peculiar to the New England rural folk. I don't know when I've spent a happier rainy Sunday.

The editor of the *Dallas News* literary page has commissioned me to write a column (or more) article on your *Collected Poems,* but it will be sometime in November before he can print it, I fear. I'll do it right away and send it in, however I'll send a copy of the review when it appears.

In reading through my volume I noted several typographical errors, or rather inconsistencies in spelling, and a few small points which you may wish to consider in preparing for later printings of the trade edition. For example, I note a number of inconsistencies in the *-or- our* words, —not all of them by any means, I imagine. I suppose the fact that you first brought out your early volumes in England—where they use the *-our* spelling preferably, while we in America use the *-or* preferably—accounts for most of these inconsistencies.

Dr. Payne then wrote pages and pages of suggested changes. For example, he questioned the pronunciation of *row* and whether "tote road" would be better than "tote-roading." Professor Payne also mentioned a graduate thesis about Frost's poetry which had been written by a student of Dr. Payne, Miss Nicholson.

Writing a reply to Professor Payne on October 27, 1930, Frost opened his letter by exclaiming what a patient and understanding friend he had way off down in Texas. Frost said he wished he had had Dr. Payne read the final proofs of his *Collected Poems.* Addressing Dr. Payne's questions and suggestions, Frost said "Rō" is the way to pronounce "row." "Tote-roading" was preferable to "tote road," Frost wrote. Frost said Miss Nicholson's book was too good to be called a thesis. Does Frost sound like an "enraged" writer in this reply? Obviously not.

The tone of Frost's letter also clearly shows Frost's debt to Dr. Payne. In the cases of Stark Young and J. Frank Dobie, as in the case of Robert Frost, Dr. Payne made suggestions for author corrections as a personal favor to each writer. The writers expressed gratitude for Professor Payne's help. Professor Payne derived satisfaction from his work for these authors. Certainly not one author paid him for the countless hours he toiled for them, looking with his finely honed proofreading talent for errors which might embarrass the authors if printed.

The severely overworked Payne had devoted an entire day to making his first list of suggested changes for Frost. On November 14, Payne sent a second list of suggested changes to Frost.

As written earlier, Frost and Dr. Payne spent several pleasant days together in the spring of 1933, three years after the reputed "corrections controversy." Payne did not offer any more suggested corrections in Frost's poems until 1936. In March, 1936, Frost wrote Dr. Payne from Harvard, where the poet was lecturing, to announce publication of a new Frost book of poems, *A Further Range.* Frost also wrote Professor Payne to tell him that he had burned two checks Payne had sent him for two volumes of his poetry. Frost said Payne could not buy his books because he liked Payne. He always sent Dr. Payne signed copies of his volumes of poetry when they were published. Frost asked Dr. Payne to set him a good example in letter writing and write him. Dr. Payne's arm did not have to be twisted to write Frost a letter, especially on invitation to do so, and Dr. Payne wrote Frost on May 2, 1936. The most important parts of Dr. Payne's letter are quoted.

"That spontaneous letter you sent me away back in March has been a source of much genuine pleasure to me since it came. I have read it over at least once a week, and now I have it almost by heart . . . I was mightily pleased to hear about the new book—*A Further Range*—and the topics of the Harvard lectures. I wish I could have heard you talk on these topics. Maybe you will compile a book of your poetry pronouncements someday.

"Mrs. Payne joins me in love to both (and all) the Frosts. I have been thinking that maybe if those northern winters are too severe on you and Elinor you might come down and spend two or three of the severest months with us. We have a room for you if you will just be home folks. And I might be able to get President Benedict to find you some sort of stipend if you would give some informal poetry talks to our students who are interested particularly in the creative side of literature. . . ."

In late May, 1936, Payne made a long list of suggested corrections for *A Further Range* and sent them to Frost. Among the words discussed were *codlin, measured* and *was measured,* and *it's* after *doubt.*

Frost's reply should be dated July 10, 1936. In his reply, Frost makes the oft-quoted statement, "But you know I indulge a sort of indifference to punctuation." Frost then concerned himself with Dr. Payne's formidable list of corrections. Frost said his use of *was measured,* though passive, was "perfectly idiomatic." Frost said *codlin'* would look funny.

Frost concluded the letter by thanking Dr. Payne for all his trouble in both proofing the book of poems and reviewing it. [Professor Payne wrote a favorable review of *A Further Range* for the *Dallas Morning News.*] Frost asked Dr. Payne what form of *A Further Range* he lacked and offered to send it to him. Frost's last words said Payne knew that Frost was always faithfully his friend. All in all, hardly an "enraged" letter from Frost.

To clarify the Thompson/Barry/Hall/Lathem confusion of the Frost letter, I reexamined the original letter in The Humanities Research Center of The University of Texas. The postmark on the envelope read July 10 followed by a blurred year date. If the year had been 1930, Frost could not have replied to an October, 1930 list of suggested corrections in July, 1930! I examined all the other Frost letters to Payne and found the dates in the letters corresponded to the postmarks on the envelopes. Dr. Payne confused the date more when he wrote notes on Frost's letter to the effect that the letter was in response to Payne's suggested corrections for *Collected Poems* of 1930. I examined the postmark on the envelope with a magnifying glass. The examination revealed the postmark to be July 10, 1936, as I had guessed. A blue pen had been used to make a circle out of the 6. The postmark had been altered. By whom? Perhaps Dr. Payne himself thought the postmark 1930 and could not see it well, and therefore drew the 0 to "clarify" the date for posterity. On the other hand, the letter had been exhibited several times at The University of Texas and someone, perhaps a student pulling a prank, altered the postmark.

Professor Payne compounded the problem in his reply to Frost's July 10, 1936 letter by misdating his own letter as July 16, 1939. Since Payne's letter directly addressed Frost's letter of July 10, 1936, and Frost wrote no other letters to Payne in the month of July in any year, Payne's letter was written in 1936, not 1939.

July 16, 1939 [sic]

Dear Robert Frost:

Your good letter of July 10 has reached me. I am glad to know that you understand the spirit in which I sent on those proof readings. You seemed to have appreciated the markings I sent you when *Collected Poems* appeared, and I thought you might want to normalize the whole thing when you came to make your final edition. I am not much of a martinet about misprinting—in fact, I claim to be a liberal down here in this ultra academic English faculty. But I am in the educational game, and I am trying to "play the game according to the rules," that's all. What the school teachers want to see is that the poets and writers whose works are put before the young readers shall be in good conventional form in order that they may have correct models before them always. One couldn't put the modern radical poets before children and expect them to be able to read them intelligently. . .

I am glad you corrected my misapprehensions about certain lines. Those were mere suggestions for polishing off—not criticisms at all. I hope you understood that. I had no notion of presuming to correct your English. I merely wanted to call your attention to some things that seemed to my eye to need some little adjusting.

You ask what form of the book I needed . . . I have the review copy of the first trade edition of *A Further Range*. . . . I need (or *crave* most *avidly*) a copy of the trade edition as a presentation copy from you—with such associational material as you have time or inclination for. I hate to impose on you, for you have already been so good to me. But I now count yours my premiere collection of all I have . . .

Mrs. Payne sends you and "Elinor" her love and says she will try to write a letter soon. We are about ready to go on a short round of visitations to our grand-children in the three Payne substations.

Please direct the books to me at the University. They will be kept there until our return.

With all my love to you and yours,

L. W. PAYNE, JR.

Professor Payne provided his version of the "corrections controversy" and summed up his relationship with Frost in "Scholarship and the Creative Writer," published in the January, 1938 issue of *Texas Outlook*. Dr. Payne based his article on an address he had made on October 7, 1937, before the Annual Academic Convention of the Texas State College for Women, Denton, Texas.

"Scholarship and the Creative Writer"
by L. W. Payne, Jr.
UNIVERSITY OF TEXAS

There are some people who believe that scholarship is inimical to creative writing, that the poet should certainly not devote his time and energy to what we usually denominate purely academic scholarship. I hold that the creative writer should himself be a good scholar, though not in the restricted academic sense of the word.

The creative writer should be a scholar in the more general conception of the word, a man who has a wide acquaintance with the best that has been thought and said in the world, not only in science and literature, but also in history and sociology and government and all those subjects or arts which we call the humanities and which deal primarily with man and his products.

The poet, or creative writer, should take that middle ground between specialized academic scholarship and that general concept of scholarship which makes him a master of words as the medium of his artistic conceptions. Books he must know as his familiar and intimate friends. He must be a great reader of the accepted masterpieces of the past and a judicious taster of the works of his contemporaries, the makers of the prospective masterpieces of his own time.

I want to bring my topic down to our own time and, if you will permit me, single out as one example of what I think is the ideal combination of scholarship and creative ability in poetry among our living American poets, namely, Robert Frost.

95

It has been my good fortune to have met Mr. Frost half a dozen or more times, to have corresponded with him for years (literally years, for it takes him about a year to answer one of my letters) and finally to have had the still greater good fortune and honor of having both Mr. and Mrs. Frost as guests in my home on two separate occasions of several days each. You can get acquainted with people if you live in the same house with them for days at a time. And how we did talk! And what a talker Frost is! He dearly loves to sit up until three o'clock in the morning talking and talking, on and on. He is like the average farmer, eager for a time to talk. Read the little poem, "A Time for Talk," to illustrate how a dirt farmer,—and Frost is really a dirt farmer you know,—takes every opportunity to have a good talk, to "visit," as he would say, with his neighbor. And what long, friendly talks we had, both pairs of us, for our wives can talk almost as much as men, you know!

Well, out of all this talk, and out of all my very close reading of everything that Frost ever wrote that I could get my eye on, I have learned a great deal about the mental habits, about the immense reservoirs of information, about his deep interest in politics, and about his wide familiarity with the great books of the world, and many of the lesser books, too, even down to the twaddle of dozens of minor poets. Frost spent the winter in Texas this past year, and while he was down here he read a considerable number of Texas books. For example, he got hold of one of W. P. Webb's books, "The Texas Ranger," and he merely made one remark to me about it: "My, what a book that is of Webb's; I never cared much for the ballads and stories about desperadoes like Billy the Kid or Sam Bass, for I always felt that there were better ballads and better stories to be written about the men that ran the desperadoes down." Now, is there not a good deal of sound common sense and even profound scholarship in that remark?

Another thing I learned was that Frost had a great deal of respect for accurate scholarship. Even as to the matter of careful proofreading he admitted he was not indifferent; but he said that sort of thing, important as it is, has never been his chief concern. He said that he would rather his publishers and friends would look after those minor matters so that he could pay more attention to the ideas and the tones of the speaking voice in his poems. He works much harder on his poems than one would think. He cares little for the mere formal matters of metrics and the rhetorical rules of composition, but he is deeply interested in the meaning of words, in their minute shades of connotation, and particularly their effectiveness in certain combinations in evoking for the reader the actual speech tones of his characters. The fact is he conceives it his chief business as a poet to capture the very essence of his subject, to probe into the very depths of the meaning of life among the simple New England farmer folk whom he knows so well by intimate contact and whom he portrays so truly and lovingly. There is no sort of doubt in my mind that this is the kind of scholarship a creative writer should possess.

Moreover Frost is a great student of human life in books as well as in the real scenes around him, but he never surrenders to the great writers of the past so far as to use them as models. He has found his own way of expressing his own ideas and inspirations, and he steadily maintains his own independence and integrity as an artist and as a student of life as he knows it. In other words Frost is both a scholar and a poet, and I might add also that he is a scholar and a gentleman, too, both in life and in letters.

Last winter I was talking with him about this matter of teaching literature, particularly poetry, and I happened to remark that I never presumed to try to make poets and creative writers out of my students, but that I was immensely pleased whenever I discovered one who wanted to write and I always took pains to encourage such a one. I finally said something like this: "You know, I must have something of the missionary spirit in my make-up, for I can't help aiming in my teaching at the 95 percent of my students who will never become savants or scholars in the academic sense of the word rather than at the 5 percent who will become scholars. The great majority of our college students will go back to their homes in the towns and cities and on the farms and ranches and make good citizens, build comfortable domiciles, and rear healthy and lovely children."

Imagine my surprise when he came up to the University last March to make just one address during his winter vacation in Texas—which, by the way, he spent hidden away in San Antonio— and announced for his subject: "The Other Ninety-Five Percent of You." I had forgotton my remark, and I could not even guess what he intended to talk about when he sent me that peculiar title. Well, he began by saying that only 5 percent of all the university students in all the colleges of the land would ever become learned men, great scholars, great investigators, or discoverers of new knowledge. The other 95 percent would go back home and live the life of normal law-abiding citizens, law-abiding for the most part at least, and out of that 95 percent would eventually come most of the poets, novelists, painters, sculptors, architects, and artists of all kinds that our nation is destined to produce. He admitted that the great universities were primarily founded for the 5 percent, but that 95 percent, the home-makers and prospective artists, were here and were grateful for the crumbs of knowledge which fell to them and which were stimulating and nutritive in one way or another toward the production of good citizens both as artisans and artists. Think that proposition through, and see if you don't agree with Mr. Frost.

CHAPTER NINE

England 1938

PROFESSOR Payne once said that everybody in America wants to go to England at least once in his life. The busy Payne made his once in his life trip to England in the summer of 1938. According to his colleague, Dr. Robert Law, Dr. Payne went to England partly to do research for a course and partly for a vacation.

Professor and Mrs. Payne made a leisurely cruise from New York on the liner *Queen Mary* in early June.

Once in London, the Paynes visited the British Museum and inspected some of its manuscripts. After several days of London sightseeing, the Paynes traveled to Stratford on Avon to visit Shakespeare's home. But Dr. Payne enjoyed most his sightseeing visit to Dorchester. Dorchester was the setting of Thomas Hardy's novels and Dr. Payne knew them well. Professor and Mrs. Payne wandered around Dorchester for three days in mid July, studying the scenes which Hardy used as settings for many of his novels. In 1944 Dr. Payne told a friend that, "My greatest regret was that I could not meet Hardy in person."

While never meeting Hardy, Dr. Payne did meet novelist Hugh Walpole and poets Walter de la Mare and Stephen Spender that summer. No record of Professor Payne's visit with Spender at Hollings Bookshop in London has survived, but Dr. Payne's visits with de la Mare and Walpole have survived in vivid detail through Dr. Payne's notes.

Professor Payne said he loved Walter de la Mare because that poet loved fairy tales and romantic tales of every kind. "De la Mare is, then," Payne said, "a poet after my own heart."

De la Mare and Payne shared the same year of birth, 1873, although de la Mare managed to be a few months older. Both men were married at 24 and by 1938, both had four children. Both had

three boys and a girl. The girl came as the third child in each sequence. Professor Payne took these comparisons seriously and
noted in 1942 that he had seven grandchildren to de la Mare's five.

The Paynes received an invitation to tea with de la Mare at Taplow for four p.m., Sunday, June 26. De la Mare usually held Sunday afternoon tea for visitors and he was very cordial to people
who expressed an interest in poetry.

The brick walls that surrounded the village of Taplow stood
eight to nine feet high, Dr. Payne estimated. The de la Mares'
hedged lane which led up to the house impressed Dr. and Mrs.
Payne and they loved the large flower garden concealed at the rear
of de la Mare's house. Dr. Payne thought the entire enclosure of
house and garden to be at least an acre.

When the Paynes arrived at de la Mares' home, Mrs. de la Mare
met them at the door. Dr. Payne described her as "a pale little lady,
not short but very thin, who walked with short mincing steps as if
she were almost an invalid." Mrs. de la Mare proved to be charming and Mrs. Payne promptly took a great liking to her. Soon the
two women were exchanging confidences with each other on their
children, grandchildren, and other household affairs. Meanwhile
Payne and de la Mare retired to the living room to talk.

Robert Frost was the one person whom both Dr. Payne and
de la Mare had entertained in their homes, and so Frost served
as the starting point for their conversation about poetry. De la
Mare asked Dr. Payne what American critics thought of Frost and
Edwin Arlington Robinson. Dr. Payne replied that the general
consensus in the academic and critical world held that Robinson
proved the greater poet. Professor Payne said that he had recently
changed his opinion in Frost's favor. Dr. Payne said Frost "was
more individual and more part and parcel of the American life."
De la Mare agreed with Dr. Payne that Frost was the greater poet.

Professor Payne's conscience perhaps bothered him a little at
this point in the conversation, for he felt it necessary to tell de la
Mare, " . . . my change of opinion was probably due to the fact I
had known Robinson only through his works and by correspon-
dences with him, while I learned to know Frost personally by
having him and his wife (and his daughter Lesley and her two

girls) in my home on two real visits, besides three or four other meetings in San Antonio and Boulder, Colorado." What Professor Payne was certainly confessing was that his literary judgment could have been influenced by friendship, by the charm of conversation with Robert Frost. The candor of this confession is remarkable. It is safe to say few critics would ever admit their judgments might be influenced by friendship. That Dr. Payne was honest enough to admit that possibility demonstrated another example of his rare integrity.

When Dr. Payne and de la Mare broached the subject of British poets, Payne asked what de la Mare thought about the new British school of poets. De la Mare avoided answering the question so Dr. Payne gathered that de la Mare did not like the modern postwar school of British poetry.

At 4:30, Mrs. de la Mare invited her guests into the dining room where she laid out a table laden with bread and butter, raisin cakes, chocolate layer cake, candies, and little sandwiches. The tea was English of two varieties, Indian and Chinese. Dr. Payne selected Indian tea.

Near the end of the day Dr. Payne asked de la Mare if he would sign his collection of works which were being assembled by Dr. Payne's agent in London, and made it clear the commercial value of books signed by de la Mare held no interest for him but their "associational value" did. Dr. Payne explained that he intended to leave his rare books and associated items to The University of Texas Library and promised the books would never come to the market for sale, even though Dr. Payne was not rich enough to give the library to the University outright since, he said, he had put a large part of his little savings into the books and he felt he ought to leave at least enough money to help in the education of his grandchildren. De la Mare joked that it would be "an enormous burden" for him to autograph copies of his books for Dr. Payne. [Dr. Payne's daughter donated substantial sums to The University of Texas to accompany the Payne Library when it was eventually left to The University of Texas. The original vision of a separate collection for Payne's books set distinctly apart from other books was never realized and today Dr. Payne's collection is interspersed with other books in the University's Humanities Research Center.]

Three days later, one of the most pleasing honors bestowed on Professor Payne in his lifetime took place by accident in London on June 29, 1938. Mrs. Payne had read a London newspaper notice announcing that on June 29 a memorial tablet to W. H. Hudson, the novelist and naturalist, would be unveiled at 40 St. Luke's Road, London, where Hudson lived for forty years until his death in 1922. Because Professor Payne was a Hudson scholar and an admirer of the Argentine writer, he and Mrs. Payne decided to attend the ceremony.

The plaque, designed by Argentine sculptor Luis Perlotti, was a gift of The Society of Hudson's Friends at Quilmes, near Buenos Aires, where Hudson had been born.

Dr. Don Manuel Malbran, the Argentine Ambassador to The Court of St. James, had planned to perform the ceremony. Approximately three hundred persons gathered at the appointed time for the unveiling, but Ambassador Malbran was not one of them. What to do? After a messenger brought word that the ambassador would not be able to attend the ceremony, Senor G. Uriburu of the Argentine Embassy unveiled the plaque. But who would deliver the address? A member of the committee in charge of the unveiling recognized Dr. Payne, the tall Texan in the audience. The member asked Dr. Payne to give a talk in place of Ambassador Malbran and Dr. Payne quickly agreed.

Speaking extemporaneously but articulately, Dr. Payne expressed the honor and pleasure he felt to represent by proxy both North and South America, for on both continents W. H. Hudson was highly revered. Professor Payne noted that Hudson's parents had migrated to Argentina from New England. Professor Payne discussed *Green Mansions* and *Far Away and Long Ago*, which Professor Payne declared Hudson's greatest works.

Typical in Dr. Payne's career, when his photograph appeared the next day, June 30, 1938, in *The Times* of London, the caption misidentified him at the unveiling as "Mr. H. R. Dent."

Seeking a change after two weeks of research, Dr. Payne joined a sightseeing tour on July 12. Riding by bus out from London, the Paynes saw Eton College, Windsor Castle and, in Buckinghamshire, on the way to Oxford, the cottage where John Milton was born.

The Paynes saw the town of Henley, where the Henley Regatta had recently been rowed and they visited Christ's Church College. At Henley, Dr. Payne noted that they saw goats from India, walking along the road, which had furnished milk for Gandhi during his recent conference in London.

The tour left Oxford at two p.m. and passed through St. Mary's Church at Banbury Cross with its beautiful Roman dome and stained glass windows. After a short visit to Warwick Castle, the tour passed Leamington, a health resort for rheumatics. The next stop was Kenilworth, where Sir Walter Scott wrote some of his novel *Kenilworth* in the Castle Hotel. The tour concluded in London with a visit to the Tower.

Professor Payne learned something new at the Tower—that the Tower actually consists of twenty buildings and towers, covering eighteen acres along the north bank of the Thames. The central White Tower, he discovered, begun in 1078 during the reign of William the Conqueror, was originally a fortress and royal residence, but later used as a prison. Professor and Mrs. Payne glanced at the Crown Jewels, closely guarded in the Tower.

The Paynes abandoned their sightseeing on August 7 for another visit to the de la Mares. After some discussion about de la Mare's American travels on the Hudson River and Chesapeake Bay, Dr. Payne turned the discussion to books. He said he had just paid $60 for a copy of de la Mare's first book, *Songs of Childhood*. De la Mare said that was a fair price, for the book often sold for much higher. Dr. Payne told de la Mare he had four books he wished him to sign but forgot to say he had brought them with him.

Continuing their discussion over tea, Dr. Payne and de la Mare moved to the subject of autobiographies. They agreed that autobiographies that concentrated on a writer's childhood were the most charming. They also agreed that their favorite autobiography was *Far Away and Long Ago* by W. H. Hudson.

Dr. Payne told de la Mare that he had been trying to get Robert Frost to write his memoirs and theories of poetry. De la Mare said, "You tell Frost for me that I had a dream which was something like this: I saw in my dream a long corridor, and far down at the end of the corridor there appeared a light, and the light glowed and grew until it formed a larger amorphous face with two bright spots in it like the flaming eyes of a poet or prophet; and the message of the figure was this: 'Tell Robert Frost that he must write an autobiography.'" Dr. Payne laughed and asked, "Did you really dream that or did you just make it up on the spur of the moment?"

"You have insulted me by doubting my veracity," joked de la Mare.

Moving right along, as the saying goes, Dr. Payne asked de la Mare why most modern poets eventually wrote novels.

"Simply because the stupid public will not buy poetry, and a poet, like other people, has to live," de la Mare answered.

When Dr. Payne left de la Mare he set to work immediately in reading the de la Mare works which he had not previously read. As was his bent, Professor Payne set down suggested corrections from the volume of de la Mare poems called *Memory*. When Payne presented the corrections, de la Mare did not see any he thought should be made, but he said he felt highly complimented that Payne had troubled himself to make the suggested corrections.

Terribly impressed by his visits with de la Mare, Professor Payne wrote in September, 1938, "On the whole I was impressed with Mr. de la Mare as a man of infinite resourcefulness, verve, and energy, a real poet whose chief love is the beauty and innocence of nature and of man in a state of innocence as in the natural and spontaneous actions and emotions of children. He is something more than a mere poet of child life, however, for he simply goes back to the age of innocence for his argument that all life should be natural and spontaneous—even as the childhood of each of us is more or less natural and spontaneous. De la Mare is perhaps one of the best poets living and writing in England today. I believe he ranks beside W. B. Yeats and perhaps he will reach even a wider public than Yeats will eventually command. Both are poets of the first rank, I think, each fine in his own individual way."

Two days after his second visit with Walter de la Mare, Dr. Payne met Sir Hugh Walpole, the great British novelist, at Walpole's bachelor chambers, 90 Piccadilly Street, London. Walpole's apartment was near Green Park, so Dr. Payne rested in Green Park for ten minutes in order to be exactly on time for his interview.

A bellboy in uniform showed Professor Payne to Walpole's quarters. Professor Payne found Walpole in his shirt sleeves on a warm summer day in London. Numerous pieces of sculpture, some of them life-size figures in various poses, surrounded Walpole, and many pictures and engravings decorated the walls. Curiously shaped and lightly colored vases rested on large book cases.

In his discussion with Dr. Payne, Walpole did not talk about technique or form, but rather gossiped about individual novelists. Walpole said that a distinct school of younger English novelists emerged in 1909 or 1910. The leading members of this new school, Walpole said, included D. H. Lawrence, E. M. Forster and himself, with Lawrence, Walpole said, the best of the three. Walpole, however, said that Lawrence overemphasized sex in some of his later works.

Saying little about himself, Walpole praised the work of Compton Mackenzie, remarking that Mackenzie was the most "literary" of his generation. Walpole particularly praised Mackenzie's novel *Sinister Street*. As an afterthought, Walpole mentioned Somerset Maugham but noted he was just a little older than Lawrence and Mackenzie.

Taking up the post-World War I novelists, Walpole praised Aldous Huxley and Virginia Woolf as the most gifted of the group emerging in the period from 1920 to 1930. He said Woolf carried very great importance.

Dr. Payne finally led Walpole into a discussion of his own works. Dr. Payne mentioned *Fortitude* and *Cathedral*. Walpole played down the fact that *Fortitude* had been a great success in America, suggesting it was an early and "callow" book and not one of the best examples of his mature writing.

Professor Payne then asked Walpole if any of the cathedrals he had seen served as a vague model for *The Cathedral*. Walpole said that if any cathedral could be said to be a model it would probably be Canterbury, though any of several cathedrals would answer for all practical purposes.

Walpole said the "Herries" series of novels, of which there were four—*Rogue Herries, Judith Paris, The Fortress, Vanessa*—provided good examples of his later period and *The Fortress* one of his best books period. Walpole suggested *Rogue Herries* might be a better novel for study purposes. Then Walpole called Dr. Payne's attention to a novel from his middle period, *The Dark Forest*, which Walpole said was a favorite of his. *The Dark Forest* grew from Walpole's war experiences at the Russian front in World War I. And Walpole thought *The Dark Forest* would be one of his works that would last the longest. Walpole told Payne *The Dark Forest* was the novel of distinctly modern significance among his works.

As a final bit of advice Walpole urged Dr. Payne to find a copy of Ernest Baker's new book *The History of the Modern English Novel*. This book would be most helpful, he said, for Dr. Payne's course on the modern English novel.

When the half hour interview ended, Walpole said he was sorry that he had to leave to catch an early afternoon train. Professor Payne put his jacket on to go but Walpole talked on. Walpole said he regretted having to break off an interesting talk on the recent novelists and new trends in fiction. And then Walpole continued talking, suggesting he might be back in America again, but not on a set lecture tour. Walpole said he would only appear in a few places where he had friends, if at all, and not under a regular manager of lectures. Dr. Payne promised Walpole a warm reception if Walpole visited Austin. Walpole replied that he would be glad to visit The University of Texas since his interest had been aroused in the university library he had heard Texas possessed. Walpole predicted that a great future lay ahead for Texas. Dr. Payne mentioned that Walpole had loaned The University of Texas unpublished letters of Sir Walter Scott. Walpole said that he had been glad to lend his Scott letters for purposes of filling out some Scott correspondence the University already owned.

Professor Payne looked upon his visit with Sir Hugh Walpole as one of the most pleasing he had ever had with a writer. Sailing home on the *Queen Mary* shortly afterwards, Dr. Payne wrote, "The fact is I have known more poets than novelists, and this contact with Walpole was really a new and altogether pleasant experience."

CHAPTER TEN

Anthologies

$\mathcal{P}$ROFESSOR Payne supplemented his income by writing anthologies, works that became basic English texts for high school students. This proved to be lucrative. In 1922, for example, Professor Payne earned in salary at The University of Texas $3250. His book royalties for the year came to $2880. His book writing nearly doubled his income. Yet Dr. Payne always worried about being able to support his growing family. Even in his later years when his children were married and financially secure, he worried about giving support to his grandchildren.

Dr. Payne's book writing became an important part of his personal life. In order to build a new addition on the house, Dr. Payne's publisher, Rand McNally in 1923, advanced him $3000. In 1936, Rand McNally reported to Payne that he would realize at least $2000 in royalties from one book alone, *Enjoying Literature*. It would be enough, Rand McNally assured him, to take his proposed trip to England, two years hence, in 1938. Rand McNally told Dr. Payne that his royalties from this one book might eventually total two or three times $2000.

In all, Professor Payne authored nine books and coauthored three other texts.

Writing anthologies required Dr. Payne to visit Rand McNally's Chicago offices. In this context, as reported earlier, Dr. Payne met Carl Sandburg when the poet was writing the first *Lincoln* book. While in Chicago, Dr. Payne usually stayed with his Rand McNally editor, E. C. Buehring and his wife. Dr. Payne enjoyed his Chicago visits greatly, calling on writers, attending the theater, taking in Carl Sandburg's kind of Chicago. In addition to visiting Sandburg, Dr. Payne called on Harriet Monroe and he attended the theater frequently when in Chicago. For example, on September

23, 1923, Dr. Payne saw "Beggar on Horseback" at the Adelphi Theatre. The next night he saw "Seventh Heaven" at George M. Cohan's Grand Opera House, featuring Jason Robards, Sr., father of the current actor Jason Robards, Jr.

Professor Payne began his career as an anthologist in 1913, corresponding with The Library of Congress to check facts and dates, a practice he continued for the rest of his life. The 1913 book, *Southern Literary Readings*, Dr. Payne felt the most affection for among all his books. He said he spent more time and energy on that book than any two of his larger books which followed.

Professor Payne brought out *Learn to Spell* in 1914, a work originally published by The University Cooperative of The University of Texas. In 1916 Rand McNally reprinted *Learn to Spell*, which divided words into categories to give some context to them: English literature, foreign languages, history, mathematics, economics, agriculture, botany, chemistry, geology, physics, physiology, zoology, education, engineering, and architecture. Dr. Payne provided thirty-five pages of words commonly misspelled and gave helpful hints such as, "In general, when two or more spellings are in use, choose the simpler or more accurately phonetic form."

Learn to Spell proved a fine book and it was well received. E. O. Sisson, Idaho's Commissioner of Education, said *Learn to Spell* surpassed everything he had read concerning the problems of spelling. Subsequently, *Learn to Spell* became widely adopted for use. In addition to Idaho's public schools, and of course Texas, the Alabama Girl's Industrial Institute adopted the textbook.

Spelling and grammar stayed close to Dr. Payne's heart. Although he took both disciplines seriously, he could joke about spelling problems. Among difficult words to spell, he noted the word *ecstasy*. "Few people know how to spell *ecstasy*," he said. "In fact, if the word got through correctly spelled, some proof reader would change it, thinking he was doing the writer a favor."

Professor Payne favored simplifying spelling and served as a member of the Executive Council and the Texas representative in the Southwest for the Reform Spelling Movement. Discouraged about the movement's failure to get anywhere, Payne wrote in

1927, "I have discovered that all the larger interests, such as publishers, the newspapers, the press in general, are wedded to the conventional system and have a great deal of money invested in it. Hence I have despaired of any radical reform coming about in our time. The only thing we can do, it seems to me, is approve the principle of simplification and look forward to a gradual reformation in our spelling."

Dr. Payne next wrote *American Literary Readings,* the first of the anthologies which he authored alone. This book provided a chronological examination of American literature, with each major period punctuated by samples of the leading authors and introduced by a short analysis by Dr. Payne. At the end of each chapter Dr. Payne posed a series of questions about the authors for students to ponder. He used this format in all of his anthologies. Published in 1917, *American Literary Readings* received critical acclaim. The *Sewanee Review* said *American Literary Readings* could be safely recommended as a basal text in American literature. Rommie R. Boyd, head of the English department of Brownwood High School, Brownwood, Texas, considered *American Literary Readings* the most notable contribution that had been made to the teaching of American literature in the high school.

Not everyone felt as enthralled with the book. University of Wisconsin Professor W. B. Cairns questioned Dr. Payne's inclusion of O. Henry's stories. Despite Professor Cairns' reservation, *American Literary Readings* became used across the nation, including the public schools in Salt Lake City.

Dr. Payne wrote *American Literary Readings* with a certain anxiety. His father, eighty years old in 1917 and in failing health, made Professor Payne particularly concerned that Rand McNally should send his father a complimentary copy. His anxiety proved to be well grounded, for Leonidas W. Payne, Sr. died in January, 1918.

In the months following his father's death, Dr. Payne worked hard on his next book, *History of American Literature.* Despite his hard labors, Dr. Payne continued to make changes in his manuscripts and by late December he had fallen behind schedule. Rand McNally became anxious. His editor Buehring sent a telegram on

December 28, 1918, saying Payne's request for an extension of time was a "serious mistake" and that Payne should come immediately to Chicago because the proofs should be read there. Instead, Dr. Payne sent suggested corrections by mail. *History of American Literature* finally came off the press in early 1919.

Letters to Professor Payne demonstrated a mixed reaction to the book. Amy Lowell, the great Boston poet, thought Dr. Payne's scheme in the book interesting but she said there were a great many errors. She said Dr. Payne had listed a number of people of very little importance, but who these people were she did not say. She said further that Professor Payne had dealt with the living poets in a superficial manner.[1] Professor Payne's friend Harriet Monroe was kinder. Monroe felt the book very good and that Dr. Payne had handled the chapter on modern poets well. Her only suggestion came in the comment that the book could stand a more complete indexing.[2] University of Alabama Dean and Professor of English C. H. Barnswell was particularly impressed that Dr. Payne had dealt mainly with the American writers of the nineteenth and twentieth centuries.

History of American Literature, like the other Payne books, received wide adoption, including adoption in the public schools in Oregon and Tennessee.

In 1921 and 1922 Professor Payne compiled and wrote *Selections from English Literature*. On July 5, 1922, Dr. Payne wrote William Butler Yeats seeking permission to use five Yeats poems for the anthology. Yeats replied on August 23, 1922, in a letter in which he remembered his 1920 Austin visit, and then referred Dr. Payne to his agents. Yeats wrote in part: "My visit to Texas is vivid in my imagination. I am sure you will forgive me for asking you to write about the anthology rights to my agents . . . I always feel very mean in asking anybody for a fee, remembering when I was a young writer I published anthologies without paying anything to anyone, but there were a few anthologies in those days and now there are many.[3] Dr. Payne eventually used five Yeats poems in his book. They were: "The Stolen Child," "The Ballad of Father Gilligan," "The Fiddler of Dooney," "The Cap and Bells," and "The Lake Isle of Innisfree."

Time pressures forced Dr. Payne and Rand McNally to seek a coauthor for *Selections*. Publisher and author agreed on Nina Hill, head of the English department in Austin High School, Austin, Texas, to help Payne; understanding that she be paid one-third of Dr. Payne's royalties, which amounted to ten percent of sales. *Selections from English Literature* appeared in the late autumn of 1922 and was widely used across America, including the public schools in Trenton, New Jersey.

In compiling *Selections from Later American Writers*, (1927) Dr. Payne contended with the sensitivities of T. S. Eliot and Edwin Arlington Robinson. Eliot wrote Professor Payne on 7 November 1927, saying he regretted that Dr. Payne had selected his poem "Cousin Nancy" for the anthology. Eliot said he considered "Cousin Nancy" an insignificant poem.[4] Robinson objected to Payne using poems from *The Children of the Night*. Robinson said he had eliminated that work from his *Collected Poems* in hopes of killing the poems from *The Children of the Night*.[5] Dr. Payne disagreed with Eliot and retained "Cousin Nancy" in the anthology. He also disagreed with Robinson about the *Children of the Night* poems, retaining those two immortal poems from the volume, "Richard Corey" and "Miniver Cheevey."

When *Later American Writers* rolled off the press, critics praised the volume. Typical of the praise came from Burton Roscoe's comments in *Bookman*. Roscoe wrote that he thought *Later American Writers* to be the best anthology of modern American prose and verse he had ever encountered. Roscoe praised the "brilliant and comprehensive" criticism and interpretation. Roscoe speculated that if all professors were like Dr. Payne, culture in America would be looking up. Dr. Payne, of course, delighted in such praise from Roscoe who had been the first critic of note to hail T. S. Eliot's "Waste Land" as a great modern work.[6]

A year later, in 1928, Dr. Payne's first anthology of Texas literature, entitled *A Survey of Texas Literature*, appeared in published form. In *A Survey of Texas Literature*, Dr. Payne discovered that much of the early writing about Texas had been done with the avowed purpose of attracting immigrants to Texas and thus the works filled with description of the soil, the climate, the flora, and fauna, and explanations of the temper of the native Indians and the attitude of the Mexican government. Professor Payne noted Col. Stephen F. Austin's *Translation of the Laws of Texas*, printed in Texas in November, 1829, represented the first document on Texas. Never shy about boosting his friends, Professor Payne said the richest primary source of information about the colonization and early history of Texas derived from Professor Eugene C. Barker's four volume compilation of Stephen F. Austin's papers. Barker's biography, *Life of Stephen F. Austin*, published in 1925, was the "best biography that has ever been written in Texas," declared Payne. Texas poet John P. Sjolander, known as the "Dean of Texas Poets" in his lifetime, wrote that Dr. Payne's comments about him in the book were the finest that had ever been written about him.

Dr. Payne's last major anthology (he would serve as coeditor for several more in the 1930s) was *Selections from American Literature* with *Selections from Later American Writers*, published in 1930. This book developed into an update of his 1919 *Selections from American Literature* and his 1927 *Selections from Later American Writers*. Professor Payne had been planning this update for a long time and had begun as early as 1925 to seek permissions for his updated version of *Selections from American Literature*. One of the first writers to respond to Dr. Payne's query for the future anthology was E. E. Cummings.

4 Patchin Place New York City July 13, 1925
Dear Professor Payne-
    Your letter of July 2nd received. I should be very glad to have the poems included in the "Selections from American Literature." My only consideration is, that whatever you include shall be typographically intact.
    Am glad you enjoyed my verdict on Chaplin. The idea of reproducing some of my non-graphic work on the screen appeals to me greatly. Accordingly I am sending you seven photographs: three, of "realistic" paintings, four of more personal ("abstract") paintings. In the case of the four, I have marked which is *up* and have also given the title ("Noise" "is" "Sound"). By "noise" I avoid—or intend to avoid—a search, on the part of the spectator, for "recognizeable" "subject-matter."

Your assumption as regards The Enormous Room is correct.

I was born October 14, 1894. Graduated from Harvard with degree of A.B. (Major in Greek)—M.A., Harvard, 1916 (English) 6 months in American army (*drafted*). Present occupations, painting and writing.

Sincerely,

E. E. Cummings

Dr. Payne's anthology work ended as it had begun, as a contributor or consultant. In 1909 he contributed several profiles to *The South in the Making*. From 1929–1936 Dr. Payne served as a consulting editor, mostly for the use of his then famous name in anthology writing.

Probably the greatest frustration for Professor Payne in writing books came from the intrusion of politics. School texts must be adopted through state governments, and textbook companies understandably lobby those state legislatures to review their books. In 1917, M. H. Duncan, Superintendent of Schools in Amarillo, Texas, refused to use Dr. Payne's *American Literary Readings* because it contained "The Luck of Roaring Camp" by Bret Harte. Professor Payne was eloquent in defending its inclusion. He wrote Superintendent Duncan that Bret Harte represented an important figure in American literature since he was the pioneer in the development of the local color story in America, and in all of English-language literature. Dr. Payne said he had picked the least objectionable of all Harte stories. He argued that "The Luck" is not an indecent story and is written in a refined and delicate way. He conceded that one character, Cherokee Sal, is a prostitute, but that her giving birth to a child in a mining town was true to life and "truth cannot be fundamentally objectionable." Dr. Payne said, "We have been too prudish and squeamish . . . in presenting these elemental matters of sex, birth, and death to our children." He added that "The Luck of Roaring Camp" was the source of a "fine and lasting moral lesson." But Duncan was neither impressed with Dr. Payne's argument nor his work as a Sunday school teacher, which Dr. Payne cited. Duncan refused to withdraw his objection and in July, 1918 Rand McNally caved in to Duncan's pressure and told Dr. Payne that "Luck of Roaring Camp" would be removed from *American Literary Readings*.

In the mid-1920s, Johnson and Company, a publishing rival to Rand McNally, worked up enough opposition to have Dr. Payne's *Southern Literary Readings* rejected by the public schools in Virginia.

CHAPTER ELEVEN

Professor Payne

*W*HEN Leonidas W. Payne, Jr. joined The University of Texas English faculty in 1906, he became a member of a small department numbering less than a dozen men. Only one, Morgan Callaway, held the title of full professor. The others, like Dr. Payne, were merely instructors.

Callaway ruled the department with an iron hand. Although he did not officially become chairman until 1910, Callaway was clearly the department boss from the moment Payne joined the ranks in September, 1906. A conservative, traditional man, Callaway disliked and had little respect for modern literature, or as Howard Mumford Jones put it, Callaway "had no use for the post-Victorian world or anything in it."[1] Mrs. Alice Cooke of Austin, who first studied under Dr. Payne and later taught with him on the English faculty said, "Callaway never let me take a course on modern literature." Joseph M. Ray, the future president of The University of Texas, El Paso, remembers Callaway from his undergraduate days at Texas "as forbidding a person I ever ran into; once I talked to a fellow-student, who while riding a train in Georgia, encountered an old, old lady who, when learning of his being a student at U. of Texas, asked if he had ever heard of a charming young fellow who left Georgia to teach English at Austin, named Morgan Callaway. We both laughed delightedly at the thought of the old bastard ever being young or charming, for God's sake.

"I once, while woolgathering and on no evidence whatsoever, wondered how as sweet and gentle a man as Dr. Payne, ever got to be a full professor, getting past Dr. Callaway. I figured out a way: Dr. Payne was too fine and highly principled ever to kiss the old man's rear end sufficiently to cajole him."

But someone other than Callaway, namely Dean of Arts and Sciences, Hanson T. Parlin, saw to it that Payne became a full professor, Ray suggested. Parlin "could twist old Callaway's tail and get his friend L. W. P. a full professorship."

Callaway, though, has a staunch defender in D. M. McKeithan, a colleague of Dr. Payne's and now Professor Emeritus at Texas. "I loved Callaway," said McKeithan. "He worked ya hard. If you came to class unprepared, he'd put his book down and say, 'let us understand each other.' Students never came to class unprepared a second time. Many who were hostile to Callaway couldn't pass his courses. He was unreasonably hard but with him it was a matter of principle. He was the most scholarly man ever in this department. Although he was a short man physically, he was impressive, a great personality. He was kind and generous where he could be. His principles called for high standards."

Callaway made his underlings wait a long time for promotion. Dr. Payne did not become a full professor until 1919.

Dr. Payne had quickly understood that his prospects for advancement at Texas were not immediate. In 1909 he looked into other job possibilities. He considered and decided against teaching at The University of the South at Sewanee, Tennessee. He applied for a position at The University of Maine, but he was unable to have a personal conference with The University of Maine's president, a requirement. He wrote Sir James Murray, editor of *The Oxford Dictionary,* inquiring about a job. Murray replied that persons were not hired from a distance, sight unseen. So Dr. Payne stayed on at Texas and the years passed. By 1920 he was regularly listed in *Who's Who in America.* When the first graduate faculty was selected at The University of Texas in 1925, Dr. Payne became one of its professors. In 1927 Dr. Payne received an invitation to become head of the English Department at Texas Tech. He chose to remain at The University of Texas and on December 9, 1944, his colleagues honored him with a grand party at the home of Dr. and Mrs. Lloyd L. Click for his thirty-nine years of service to The University of Texas.

In addition to teaching regular courses, Dr. Payne served as chairman of a remedial committee on English for ten years, enforcing a strict graduation requirement, and he taught a special course for engineers. Professor McKeithan served with Dr. Payne on the remedial committee. "Payne would say, 'You catch em and I'll skin em.' We'd go to professors and ask for students' exam papers, such as in history, look at them for writing. That's what Payne meant when he said, 'You catch em and I'll skin em,'" McKeithan said.

"He was a great one to stress composition," added McKeithan. "He thought you could judge a strong mind from strong writing."

McKeithan said that Dr. Payne once had an assistant named Malcom Foresman who created a test composed of multiple choice and fill-ins. "Payne was angry," McKeithan said. "Students had to learn how to write, he said. Payne eliminated the test immediately."

Dr. Payne organized and for five years headed the Division of Correspondence Instruction in the Department of Extension. He initiated a plan of supplying women's clubs around Texas with regular study programs under the direction of members of the University faculty.

The organizer Payne, also became a joiner, and he belonged to The Modern Language Association, Texas Institute of Letters, American Association of College Professors and, as previously mentioned, The American Dialect Society, American Folklore Society, and Texas Folklore Society.

During his thirty-nine-year tenure, Dr. Payne taught almost every summer. If he could not be found in residence in Austin, he could probably be found at The University of Alabama, University of Colorado, University of Southern California and other universities.

Professor Payne certainly labored at many tasks. The fall semester of 1927 provides a good example. In addition to teaching three regular courses, he worked as Chairman of the Committee on Student's use of English, the remedial program. He served on the Committee on Fellowships and the Committee of Professors of English, a committee weighed down with budget considerations and new appointments to make. Professor Payne wrote twelve reviews for such publications as *The Dallas Morning News, Southwest Review,* and *Interscholastic Leaguer.* The reviews included a look at *A Dictionary of Modern Usage*, Yeats' autobiography, and E. E. Cummings' poem "Him." Dr. Payne wrote two other articles and delivered two speeches and ten lectures throughout Texas, including at Baylor University, Oak Cliff High School in Dallas, and San Marcos Academy. In addition, he did research on "Interrelations of Hardy's Poetry and Fiction."

When it came to classroom technique, Dr. Payne said the best means of securing an intimate knowledge of any selection was by the question and answer method in class, followed by a quiz on the selection.

Mrs. Jack Gray took Dr. Payne's English Prose and Poetry class. She declared Dr. Payne "thorough and demanded minute details on quizzes." Like many professors, Dr. Payne talked about enjoying literature for its own sake, but his quizzes and exams, if this exam for English 230 in the fall of 1921 is a good example, proved highly technical.

I. Discuss the elements of contrast and parallelism in Macaulay's style; consider the larger massing of material as well as the minuter elements of parallelism.

II. Draw a contrast between Macaulay's and Carlyle's diction and habits of sentence structure.

III. Discuss Macaulay's use of decorative allusions and illustrations and Carlyle's rich use of figures of speech, illustrating in each case by specific examples.

IV. Discuss briefly Carlyle's and Macaulay's use of satire and invective.

V. a. Point out and summarize the climax chapters in each of the three books of *Sartor Resartus*.

   b. Point out three chapters which prove the coherence and unity of the book as a whole.

VI. Discuss briefly Carlyle's teachings on war and duelling, obedience, heroes, works of art, work: Quote some passages in your discussion.

To bring relevance to the question and answer quizzes in class, Dr. Payne showed photographs of the authors he discussed. He also liked to show his students autographed copies of first editions of the authors discussed. Because of this, he became a prolific book collector, scrimping and saving to buy books that would help him teach more effectively. He would often stroll into class with a new book and declare, "Here's my wife's new coat," or "Here's our new rug," meaning of course that sacrifices were made to collect the valuable first editions.

In addition to showing his rare books to classes during school hours, he tried to arrange at least one party every semester at his home so that students could see his collection. Professor Payne started his book collection in 1912 when he made the selections for his anthology of Southern Literature. Madison Cawain, a Kentucky poet, sent him an inscribed copy of his poems. Dr. Payne started collecting books more systematically in 1927.

Early first editions in his collection included *The Way of All Flesh* (which Dr. Payne lost) by Samuel Butler, *The Sketchbook* by Washington Irving, *Life on the Mississippi* by Mark Twain, *The House of Seven Gables* by Nathaniel Hawthorne, *The Woodlanders* by Thomas Hardy, and ten American and three English first editions of Conrad including *The Nigger of the Narcissus.*

Dr. Payne possessed a complete set of Hardy works, thirty-seven volumes, the first volume signed by Hardy. Once valued at $600, the volumes are now priceless. In his lifetime, Dr. Payne probably had the best collection of first editions and limited editions of Frost, Sandburg and Edwin Arlington Robinson in the Southwest. As of 1940, Dr. Payne had 185 items in his Frost collection. He considered his most valuable book to be Edwin Arlington Robinson's *The Torrent and the Night Before*, first published by Robinson himself for $52 in 1896, as a surprise for his mother. And, Dr. Payne at one time was said to have the largest collection of the works of Walter de la Mare in America.

Professor Payne put many of his books on the reserve reading list in the University library. He anticipated giving the student a thrill when the student opened a book of Frost poems to read and found Frost's autograph. For English 336, for example, in 1937, Dr. Payne put fifteen such books on reserve for the class to read.

Yet Dr. Payne did not limit the class' exposure to his autographed books. For English 35, Dr. Payne required his students to look at letters sent him from Robert Bridges, England's poet laureate, Robert Frost, A. E. Housman, Nicholas Vachel Lindsay, Amy Lowell, Edgar Lee Masters, Edwin Arlington Robinson, Carl Sandburg, W. B. Yeats, Samuel McChord Crothers, and John Galsworthy.

By March 1936, Dr. Payne calculated he possessed eighty-four letters from fifty authors. Among the letters he possessed were ones from Conrad Aiken, James Branch Cabell, Hamlin Garland, William Dean Howells, Judd Mortimer Lewis, Edwin Markham, H. L. Mencken, Christopher Morley, H. G. Wells, and William Allen White. Dr. Payne often quoted from these letters and read passages from his rare books in class.

No professor encouraged his students more than Dr. Payne to attend lectures on or near campus by the literary greats, such as the address given at Gregory Gymnasium on the University campus, November 14, 1940, by H. G. Wells. Dr. Payne liked Wells so much he had gotten special permission from University president Homer P. Rainey to hear Wells speak in Dallas the week before.

Professor Payne's national reputation as an exceptional teacher of American literature meant others often sought his advice. In February, 1938, for example, John Crowe Ransom, the great poet who had once taught with Dr. Payne at The University of Texas, wrote Payne seeking advice about two courses he planned to teach in summer school that year at Texas. For an undergraduate fiction course, Ransom, who regularly taught at Kenyon College, asked whether it would be a good idea to use two books as the text and then let students do their own reading and reporting from the library. Ransom said he would follow Dr. Payne's advice.

As a near-legend in Texas education circles, Dr. Payne came in great demand as a speaker across Texas. In 1927 his usual fee consisted of $25 and expenses. One lecture given by Dr. Payne occurred in February, 1918 at the Court House in Victoria, Texas. Dr. Payne lectured on Texas writer O. Henry, a writer of whom he spoke for one and a half hours, and when he finished, the fire had almost smouldered out in the large heating stove. According to a reporter who covered the lecture, no one in the audience moved and Dr. Payne came out of the court sanctum to greet the entire audience which quietly walked toward him. They surrounded him and listened to him chat for another fifteen minutes.

After Dr. Payne had spoken at Texas A&M in November, 1926, he received a letter of appreciation from the head of the Department of Marketing Finance, who commented Dr. Payne's lecture had aroused more interest and discussion than had been aroused on the A&M campus in a great while.

Professor Payne was especially in great demand as a speaker at graduations, said D. M. McKeithan. "Baylor President Pat Neff told me they had been especially impressed when Payne spoke at a Baylor commencement," said McKeithan. Dr. Payne also gave lectures over radio station KUT, Austin.

Decades have passed since Dr. Payne's students last saw him in class, were last inspired by his endless enthusiasm and warm demeanor. Yet the decades have not dimmed their love and admiration for Dr. Payne, who taught them to love and cherish the literature of their native land. Dr. Payne's personal attention, his kindness to each and every individual student made a lasting impression that is shown in the fond stories his former students shared with the author.

Mrs. Thomas F. Hughes, who eventually settled in Beaumont, Texas, said, "I had only one English course from Dr. Payne, English 35, I believe, but it was a revelation. I have read insatiably all my life, but in a pretty helter-skelter way, and the insight he gave me into the great writers we studied has given me life-long pleasure."

"Literature became alive," said another former student, Mrs. John B. Stigall of Dallas. "You knew that it was no prepared lecture you were hearing but rather a sharing of his great love of literature. His classes were never a study in boredom. Indeed it was exciting."

"I can remember him standing up there before the lecture section with his eyes burning with excitement about Nathaniel Hawthorne," reminisced Margaret Cousins, a noted novelist and magazine editor. She had enrolled in one of Dr. Payne's American literature courses. "He made Nathaniel Hawthorne so desirable to

121

know that I could scarcely wait to get to the library. In fact, he made all American writers exciting, and gave me my first sense of pride in our literary heritage. I still read Emerson and Thoreau with pleasure and profit, and I give him full credit. When Dr. Payne referred you to a book, it was not because he wanted you to study your lesson, but because he wanted to share what he had discovered with a friend. I consider this the crux of all teaching."

A good example of Dr. Payne's individual kindness to students is illustrated in the case of Mrs. Hallie Barton of Austin who had been sent home from the University with mumps her senior year with only two weeks remaining before the Christmas holidays. And, she had a Shakespeare paper due in Dr. Payne's class. Dr. Payne "not only sent me the book I needed but gave me the month of January to complete the paper," she said.

Miss Maud Anderson of Dallas enjoyed Dr. Payne's supportive attitude toward his students. "I appreciated the fact," she said, "that when a student did an especially good paper, he took the time to write a note to express his commendation for the work." Dr. Payne wrote such a note to Miss Anderson after she received an "A" for a paper on *Moby Dick*.

A. R. Stout, now a judge in Waxahachie, Texas, told a story that demonstrates how Professor Payne participated in his students' humor while leading them into his world of literature. "I remember one incident which drew a rare and sound laugh from him and a louder one from the class then in the old building (1918 or 1919). A rather effeminate male student was attempting to describe the 'Wife of Bathe.' Among other things, he said that she rode a red horse. It developed that he made his startling discovery from the words, 'Hir hosen were of fyn scarlet reed,' which brought down the house among the students and even the teacher did not restrain his mirth.

"When we were studying Shakespeare," Judge Stout said, "he reminded us of a Shakespearian play that was to be acted in the old (Hancock, I believe) opera house. He urged all who could afford it to attend and quoted the prices, which were reasonable. I sat in the first balcony and sometime during an intermission he looked around, apparently to see who was there. I was right behind and he seemed to reflect a look of pleasure and approval. One of our questions on our examination was in regard to the play in question, it being the one we were studying."

Dr. Payne's surviving colleagues of The University of Texas who worked with him daily, who experienced his day-to-day frustrations and successes, offered another dimension to Dr. Payne.

"Payne was kind to me when I first came," Willis Pratt said. "I wanted to teach poetry. He saw that I got a section of his modern poetry course. We taught poetry the first term of the course and the modern novel the second term. I often went in to talk to him. You were pretty free to do what you wanted.

"Once I told him I'd start with Hardy's *Tess of the d'urbervilles*, The Story of a Good Woman. He looked disturbed and he said, 'Now we all know that is his finest novel. So far not one of us has brought himself to teach it.' Finally he said, 'All right, if you want to teach it, you are free to do so.'

"Payne opened up modern poetry," Pratt said. "Callaway ruled the roost and was very conservative. Callaway thought Payne was going pretty far in teaching these new poets. In a sense, for those days he was far out by those standards."

Professor Joe Jones, author of *Life on Waller Creek*, met Dr. Payne in Lincoln, Nebraska, in the summer of 1934, when Dr. Payne visited Louise Pound, friend and fellow member of the American Dialect Society.

"Payne was instrumental in my coming to The University of Texas," Jones said. "I was working part-time at Colorado Agricultural College, now called Colorado State University. I wrote Payne asking if there were any openings at Texas. Payne said there were. I came down to Austin at my own expense. Payne was on the committee that hired new instructors and I was hired.

"Payne had a rough time with some of the English profs at UT because he taught American literature," Jones said. "He was thought to be a light-weight because of this. Payne complained to me he had not been well treated because of that on many occasions."

However, D. M. McKeithan considered such talk that Dr. Payne was looked down upon for teaching American literature "erroneous." McKeithan did know some professors resented privately Dr. Payne's extra income from writing. Despite that, McKeithan said, "As far as I know Payne didn't have enemies."

To teach in a large state university, particularly at Texas, where politics is as much a part of the air as hydrogen and oxygen, and not generate enemies, required a special talent. Dr. Payne largely channeled his energies into his love of literature. But that is not the whole story. Any man who could successfully bring back J. Frank Dobie to The University of Texas to an English Department which disliked Dobie, as Dr. Payne did, possessed no small diplomatic skills.

Dr. Payne did not spend most of his time though in campus diplomacy. He spent most of his time engrossed in his love of stories. And he loved to tell stories too.

"Payne was a marvelous story teller," said Jones.

Cornell-educated Willis Pratt, who found Southern ways a new experience, remembers Dr. Payne's stories during Sunday socials, events which young professors like Pratt were expected to attend. "Payne and many of the other professors were southerners and they took the social occasions seriously. Serious discussions on contemporary poetry would be led by Payne as he held forth, talking about his most recent letter from this or that poet," said Pratt.

Joseph Ray, in his role as Dr. Payne's typist, remembers that "once Dr. Payne had me making some stencils which traced the plot of Joseph Conrad's novel, *Lord Jim*, from the beginning of the book through the denouement to the end. He charted the novel plots and then wrote words along the side to tell about the development of the plot. I was deeply involved in this typing job when he came into the office, and I told him I was very much intrigued by it. He became deeply involved in telling me about the plot, giving me much more than the chart revealed, when suddenly he snapped his fingers and said, 'Joe, I have sat here talking to you and missed my class.'

"We examined the time and found that it was a quarter past the hour. He had become so deeply immersed in our talk, nevertheless, that he resumed it and some hour later, he snapped his fingers again and said, 'Joe I have missed my other class!' He made me promise never to tell the story, and I never did until after his death."

Dr. Payne's first heart attack in 1942 and the death of his youngest son, John, in 1943, brought shocks to Payne from which he never recovered. "He was not strong after that," his daughter Sarah said.

In the fall of 1943, the University administration put Dr. Payne on half time service. His health steadily declined and Alice Cooke, by now a professor at Texas, assisted Dr. Payne.

"He wasn't physically able to do so" [teach], Cooke said. "He was always late, didn't have time to go over notes; he often repeated lectures or gave lectures not related to the course. So I tried to keep him on track. I tried to protect him from his infirmity. I told students they were lucky to have such a wonderful teacher of literature."

Professor Payne's health deteriorated rapidly. Ellen Brodnax of Fulton, Texas had come to know Dr. Payne well in a small class he taught on Conrad. Accidentally Ellen met Dr. Payne near the end of his life. When "I was back on the campus I met Dr. Payne face to face in the hall on the ground floor of the Main Building one afternoon. He did not recognize me, and when I realized that he seemed disoriented, I did not stop and tell him who I was lest it embarrass him. He turned this way and that and then came up to me to ask the way to the elevators—the same elevators I had seen him walk so briskly to on his way to the classroom just a few years before."

Tired and disoriented, Dr. Payne yet pushed on in his teaching right up to the end, driven by a sense of duty. From his last office, room 1706 in the Main Building, Dr. Payne could peer down from his seventeenth story perch and look east at Memorial Stadium, Waggener Hall, and Gregory Gymnasium.

"His last worry in life," said his friend Robert A. Law, "was that he was unable to attend his final examination for English 35, a class that he had taught faithfully up to examination day."

"As a rule students did not love their teacher," said Alice Cooke.

"They loved Payne. He was in a class by himself. He made students understand and love literature. He made students have enthusiasm. Dr. Payne will never be forgotten by people who had him in class."

"Dr. Payne was, I think," Joseph Ray said, "the finest man I ever knew; he was straight-forward, honorable, kind-hearted, loyal to his friends—amongst whom I was proud to be numbered—and the most literate person I was ever privileged to be associated with."

"I loved the man," said Joe Jones.

CHAPTER TWELVE

The Quiet Life

L W. Payne, Jr. was, as Robert A. Law put it, "a clubbable man." Less than two months after his arrival in Austin in 1906, Dr. Payne was elected to The University Club. He eventually served terms as president of The University Club and the Fortnightly Club of Austin. He worked actively in the local Town and Gown Club and also as a Mason. Yet, the deeply religious Dr. Payne could still be one of the boys. During some unwinding at the Town and Gown Club with Dobie, Payne once humorously proposed that there should be a collection of privy poetry.[1]

In 1894 Payne had founded the Upsilon chapter of Pi Kappa Alpha at Alabama Polytechnic. He tried to start a Pi Kappa Alpha chapter at The University of Texas and ran into several obstacles. R. E. Hardaway, Jr., class of 1914, and still living in May, 1982 in Columbus, Georgia, at age 92, remembered working with Dr. Payne to get a Pi Kappa Alpha chapter at UT. Hardaway said that the Pi Kappa Alpha Board in Nashville turned down their application because he and most of the applicants from The University of Texas were engineers. Professor Payne said other fraternities represented an additional barrier because their members put up a strong fight in the Texas legislature against Pi Kappa Alpha. Not until March 1, 1920, six years after Hardaway's graduation, was The University of Texas granted a chapter of Pi Kappa Alpha.

M. P. S. Spearman, a physician living in El Paso, Texas, fondly remembers Dr. Payne's association with Pi Kappa Alpha. "Back in the years 1927–28 Dr. Payne would, several times a year, take dinner with his brothers at the old Pi Kappa Alpha house on Rio Grande. After dinner the brothers and their dates would adjourn to the drawing room, seat themselves on the floor and listen to Dr. Payne tell stories and read and discuss poetry. His podium

127

was the largest, most comfortable lounge chair in the room. For hours, before a roaring fire, on blustery winter nights, he held his audience wide-eyed and spellbound with his soft, beautiful eloquence. Often a delighted smile formed on his face, as he would note some expression of pleasure or sudden comprehension on the countenances of his listeners. So thus did this great teacher awaken in many of us a regard, possibly in some, a love, of the uses of the English language.

"This, then, was a part of my college education. Down through these many years past, I have been grateful for having listened to the beloved Dr. Payne. The memory is still warm."

Among Professor Payne's best friends were Professor L. L. Click and Dean H. T. Parlin. The Paynes and Clicks entertained each other in their homes often. D. M. McKeithan remembers seeing Dr. Payne and Parlin together at concerts. But Dr. Payne liked to unwind outdoors too.

The relaxation of fishing was particularly agreeable to Professor Payne. His fishing partners and close friends were Eugene C. Barker, the historian, and R. H. Baker, the insurance tycoon.

Like Payne, Barker had earned his Ph.D. from The University of Pennsylvania. As mentioned previously, Barker had generated recognition as the biographer of Stephen F. Austin. A year younger than Payne, Barker lived on San Gabriel Street in Austin, not far from Payne. The Paynes looked upon Barker and his wife as "our most congenial and intimate neighbors and friends."[2]

Retired English professor D. M. McKeithan remembers Barker as a man of "two personalities." Socially, Barker was a kind and gentle man, McKeithan said, but in his later years Barker became an emotional right-winger. "He hated Roosevelt, Hitler and Mussolini," McKeithan said. "He said he wanted to drown all three in the Atlantic Ocean." McKeithan recalled the time Barker blew up at a faculty meeting at the liberal Professor Ayres, calling Ayres "wet behind the ears." As one might imagine, Barker hated Roosevelt's New Deal. Barker once told historian Henry Commager that Commager's support for the New Deal was "thoughtless enthusiasm." And Barker was very pessimistic about England's chances during World War II. He wanted a quick peace for England with Germany because he felt England could not resist the Nazis. He felt that America's entrance into World War II would "bring the collapse of America's republican form of government."[3] Yet in the controversial Rainey firing by the regents Barker proved to be more of a moderate. Barker disagreed with Rainey's firing (Rainey was fired for defending academic freedom) but thought University President Rainey had challenged the regents in a way in which they had to fire him.[4] What Professor Payne thought of these issues or Barker's opinions is unknown, for as McKeithan said, "I don't remember Payne ever talking about politics. If he had strong beliefs, he hid them well."

While many disagreed with Barker's politics, most thought him a great historian. McKeithan said, "Barker was a greater historian than Webb. Even Ayres called him a great historian," McKeithan said. Today Barker's reputation as a historian is recognized by the Eugene C. Barker History Center at The University of Texas, a resource used extensively by author James Michener for his epic novel *Texas*. Barker recognized the debt to his friend L. W. Payne, Jr. in the preface to Barker's most famous book, *The Life of Stephen F. Austin*, in which Barker thanked Dr. Payne for reading the galley proofs.

R. H. Baker, Dr. Payne's other fishing partner, was a man of almost legendary dimensions. In his youth he had worked as a traveling salesman, grocery clerk, baggage master on the Yazoo and Mississippi Valley Railroad, shoe store owner, and manager of a cottonseed oil mill. His jobs carried him from his native Memphis to Arkansas and Texas. In 1887 Baker started selling insurance, which eventually proved to be his calling. He learned the trade with the Provident Life Insurance Company in Waco and then worked unsuccessfully trying to sell insurance in San Francisco, a then sparsely settled territory. He lost his capital and moved to Fort Worth in 1892 and in 1897 was appointed Texas General Agent for Equitable Life Insurance Company of New York. Baker moved to Austin that year. Baker gave up his insurance business to serve as president of the Trinity and Brazos Valley Railroad for six years and then joined the staff of Texas Governor Sayres.

During World War I Baker conceived the idea of a fishing club on Bull Creek, near Austin. As a fellow member of Payne's University Baptist Church, Payne knew Baker through his work in the building of The University Baptist Church at 2100 Guadalupe, Austin. Baker also raised funds to build the Austin Y.W.C.A.

In 1925 Baker and his son Burke organized the tremendously successful Seaboard Life Insurance Company of Houston, in which both Payne and Barker invested. American General eventually bought The Seaboard Life Insurance Company, said Mrs. George Marsh of Austin, Baker's niece.

In contrast to the other areas of his life, Baker's talents as a fisherman were rather modest. After Eugene Barker picked up Dr. Payne and Baker, since Dr. Payne did not drive, and drove out to Bull Creek, the three pals at least got a lot of fresh air. Dr. Payne good naturedly described Baker the fisherman: "I can say that he is by all odds the most patient, the most persistent, the most long-suffering fisherman I have ever known. He can sit on the big rock at Bull Creek and fish for five hours and never catch a fish. He gets more 'good bites' and catches fewer fish than any man I ever heard of. At the end of the day's sport I usually ask him how many he has caught, and he invariably replies 'I had four or five good bites but they all got away!'" Comparing his fishing to Baker, he said, "If I could get as many 'good bites' as he does, I could feed all Austin with fish, but the trouble with me is I don't even get the bites, to say nothing of the fish." Despite Dr. Payne's modesty, history shows that he caught two four-pound catfish in July, 1922.[5] D. M. McKeithan recalls that Dr. Payne, much to his delight, sometimes chartered a fishing boat near Corpus Christi, and iced the fish as he caught them.

Other pastimes of Dr. Payne's included chess and dominoes. Professor Payne usually played chess at the Faculty Club and played dominoes with neighbors. Mrs. Lewis Southerland of Austin, whose father played dominoes with Dr. Payne, remembers, "Dad and Payne were evenly matched. One night after Payne had lost, he said, 'Brains play no part in this game.'"

No matter how busy, though, Dr. Payne always made time for church. "The Church is the balance wheel of civilization," he said once.

The converted Methodist helped found and for almost forty years served as a deacon and on The Board of Deacons of The University Baptist Church in Austin. Dr. Payne taught a popular Bible as Literature class for the Sunday School and often invited his students from that class to his home for Sunday dinner.

Mrs. Margaret Burns, historian of The University Baptist Church, provided the following important dates in Payne's long association with the church:

September 9, 1909–Dr. Payne ordained

October 17, 1908–Dr. Payne elected a deacon and member of the Board of Trustees

1912–Dr. Payne elected to Bible Chair

1913–Dr. Payne looked into need for a larger church

1913–1915–Dr. Payne was Superintendent of the Sunday School

November 18, 1920–Dr. Payne read the history of the church at the laying of the cornerstone for the new building.

D. M. McKeithan recalled that Dr. Payne did not always follow the *Baptist Quarterly* when teaching Sunday School and because of that he was asked to resign from teaching his class in the mid-1930s by the pastor. "He was terribly hurt," said McKeithan.

Nevertheless Dr. Payne continued with the church in his usual noncomplaining manner and today he is remembered by the Payne Library located in the annex building behind the church sanctuary at 2100 Guadalupe. Mrs. Willa Graysner, who manages the library, said that only about ten to fifteen of Payne's original books remain in the library. The library purchases approximately twenty-five new books a year, she said, with financial support from Dr. Payne's daughter.

In 1933, Dr. Payne summed up his feelings about the importance of the Bible. "The Bible has frequently been denominated the greatest book in the world. It is more than a book—it is a library, the cream of the religious, poetic, philosophic, historical, and wisdom literature of a marvelous ancient race, the Hebrews, plus the life and sayings of the greatest product of that race, even Him who is the fulfillment of prophecy, the promised Redeemer, the Son of Man and of God. It is the greatest book in the world because it contains the profoundest truths, the sanest moral and ethical philosophy ever vouchsafed to men. It is the greatest book in the world because it is the most beautiful of all books. From the literary point of view the Bible surpasses all other books in beauty, in substance, and influence on other books."[6]

Dr. Payne made time for his children, whether in an evening of music, as his daughter Sarah Payne Foxworth remembers, when she played the piano and her father sang and played the flute, or Payne spent time out of doors. "Dad was an outdoor person," Mrs. Foxworth said. "He particularly liked to walk across Shoal Creek." At Christmas, Professor Payne gathered the children to select the Christmas tree from their lot covered with cedar trees in South Austin.

"Payne was great to Sarah's friends," said Mrs. George Marsh. "He went for hikes and picnics on Sunday almost weekly. We often went to what is now Reed Park. One time we walked across the railroad trestle over the Colorado River to Barton Springs. Mrs. Payne would have died if she had known.

"When I was twelve," Mrs. Marsh recalled, "Dr. Payne said, 'let's you and I trade birthdays. Someday somebody may believe you were my age but nobody would believe I were your age.'"

As he worked in his upstairs study at home, Dr. Payne put up with a lot of noise, his daughter said, although she knew that her mother shielded her father from outside intrusions while he worked at his desk. "Mother was a mother hen to my father," Payne's daughter said. "She protected him."

Mrs. Payne's day always began early because Professor Payne rose early. Mrs. Payne set the household tasks into operation as Dr. Payne worked in his upstairs study before breakfast. The best fig tree in Austin, with the sweetest figs, lived in the backyard at 2104 Pearl Street and provided breakfast figs often served with thick cream. After a breakfast prepared by Ethel, the Paynes' cook, Dr. Payne collected his work to head for the University and on more than one occasion walked absentmindedly toward the door on a rainy morning before Mrs. Payne could stop him to place an umbrella in his hand.

Since the Paynes ate their big meal in the middle of the day, as did most Austinites in those days, Dr. Payne usually returned home at noon, though historian Nettie Lee Benson remembers seeing Dr. Payne lunching a few times in the Student Union.

Professor Payne maintained a large appetite until his heart attack in 1942, his daughter said.

A delicious dessert at the Paynes consisted of angel food cake scooped out and filled with custard, whipped cream and strawberries. In the heat of the summer, Mrs. Payne had a particular affection for watermelon.

Dr. Payne frequently napped after his midday meal and then worked in his upstairs study. Both his daughter Sarah and his typist Joe Ray said that Dr. Payne only returned to the University if he had an appointment.

Mrs. Payne, an avid book reader whom Mrs. Hallie Barton remembers as "gracious and lovely," was the major force in the Payne home. "She planned ahead. She was a very organized lady," said Mrs. Lewis Southerland, a neighbor who spent a great amount of time with Mrs. Payne.

Mrs. Payne was called "Miss Sue" by everybody and she loved it. However, Mrs. Payne preferred that her grandchildren call her Mimie because that is what her mother, Sarah Higgins Bledsoe, was called back in Alabama. "She wanted the grandchildren to call Dad 'Papa' because that is what she called her father," Sarah Foxworth said. "But my parents called each other Darce and Dilce, Italian endearments. Then the oldest grandchild put the two together and said 'Papa-Darce,' which all the rest adopted."

The staunch Baptist Mrs. Payne allowed no liquor or cards in her household. "Nevertheless Mrs. Payne didn't object to her children dancing," Miss Sue's daughter-in-law Marietta said.

Smoking did not excite Mrs. Payne either, particularly women who smoked. Edna St. Vincent Millay "horrified" Mrs. Payne with her smoking of black cigars, said Mrs. Jack Gray, a family friend. Despite Mrs. Payne's opposition to cards, Mary Campbell of Austin remembers receiving plastic cards one Christmas from her.

Mrs. Lewis Southerland, a contemporary of Payne's youngest

133

child, John, felt close to the family with whose son she played red rover, hide and seek, marbles, and rode a pony owned by a boy in the neighborhood. Mrs. Southerland spent a great deal of time with and developed a great admiration for Mrs. Payne. "I used to sun my baby on her front porch. Miss Sue loved babies. Miss Sue would sit on her front porch and read letters or sit and rock with Mrs. Huberick, a neighbor. They would talk about their children. I remember we would have chocolate ice cream sodas every Tuesday."

Mrs. Southerland remembers that Miss Sue took charge in the neighborhood if anyone needed cheering up or congratulating. Miss Sue would organize gifts for the ill and for the postman.

"She was a darling person. So intelligent," said Mrs. Southerland. "She had a wonderful sense of humor and she laughed a lot. I just adored her."

The four Payne children each became successful in their endeavors. Probably to Dr. Payne's relief, at least in economic concerns, none of his children chose teaching as a life time career. His daughter Sarah did teach briefly at Southern Methodist University.

Dr. Payne's oldest child, William Carey Bledsoe Payne, known as "Bledsoe" and "Slim" to close friends, fought in World War I as a fighter pilot in the Signal Corps. In 1928, after graduation from The University of Texas, Bledsoe became a pilot for American Airlines. During World War II, he returned to the military to fly for the Air Transport Command, then resumed his career with American Airlines after the war, becoming operations manager for American's Nashville office. Like his father, Bledsoe converted from his given religion. He chose to be a Catholic. Bledsoe died of a stroke in 1956.

The Paynes' second child, Leonidas Warren Payne, III, was born in 1906. After graduation from The University of Texas Medical School in Galveston, Warren moved to Cleveland to intern and remained in the Cleveland area to practice medicine. Only service as a captain in the Army Air Corps during World War II interrupted Warren's distinguished forty-year medical career in Lake County, Ohio, near Cleveland. L. W. Payne, M.D. was respected and loved in his community, and became a noted hospital fundraiser. He always called his parents on his own birthday to thank them for their loving care and concern. His sister Sarah said, "He seemed to have the same feeling for his patients that his father had for his students."

Warren's sister, the Payne's third child, was everybody's joy. Born in January, 1910, Sarah Payne was adored by her family, friends, and the likes of Stark Young.

Hope Yager, a friend of the Paynes' from church, told this story about the young Sarah Payne: "When Sarah was seven her mother asked me to take her for a week to our farm twelve miles north of Austin near Dessau. The first night as twilight came, Sarah wanted to go home. I explained that my brother had the car and would not be back until late, but I promised to take her early in the morning. When morning came, she had lost any desire to go. She said in later years, 'I learned from that experience to always sleep on your problems. They usually improve overnight.'"

Sarah Payne was graduated with honors from The University of Texas in History, received her Masters in Psychology from Columbia University, and taught for one year at Southern Methodist University. She married Jack Foxworth in 1932 and gave up teaching.

There was something different about the Paynes' youngest child, perhaps even fated. John Howard Payne, born in 1913, must have grown up with a sense of rebellion against academics. Maybe an incident at age one, which dramatized his father's absentmindedness, played a part.

Professor Payne was wheeling his infant son down a sidewalk on 22nd Street in Austin while reading a book. The baby carriage got away and began rolling, Dr. Payne continued reading, unaware of the runaway carriage. Fortunately, Mrs. Payne, across the street, yelled to her husband, who recovered in time to grab the carriage.

Hope Yager recalled an incident when John was quite young. "The children of the Junior Department (of The University Baptist Church) were being entertained one hot summer afternoon and the teachers were fixing refreshments on a table under a tree. Talk of germs was quite a topic of interest and Mrs. Payne was one who tried to apply every law of cleanliness. She questioned the cleanliness of one child and was warning all the helpers to be sure his cup didn't get mixed with anybody else's. The boys came in hot and sweaty from a ballgame. Seeing the cold lemonade, John didn't wait to be served, but stuck his sweaty face into the tub and drank. The chagrin of his mother was indeed great."

Added Yager, "Friends of the family who lived next door were ever fearful that when they went to pick up their milk in the morning the cream would be missing—compliments of John or Warren."

John Payne was a natural athlete, not a natural scholar, and became a champion golfer at The University of Texas. When John flunked out of The University of Texas Law School, he explained his flunking to fraternity brother Jack Gray this way: "You know the story of the preacher's son who was the meanest boy in town. Well, my father was a professor."

John Payne found his vocation to be the same as his older brother Bledsoe. In fact, the three Payne brothers flew in World War II. John attended flying school and then married Austin beauty Marietta McGregor, whose many memories included his skills as a wonderful dancer. World War II interrupted their life together. While leading an attack on the Italian fleet supplying Rommel's African forces, John was killed on January 11, 1943. He was awarded the Medal of Honor and the airfield in Cairo named for him.

What strikes one when examining the Payne family correspondence is the closeness of the family. The sons' letters to their mother were really love letters, as they poured out their adoration for her, and reflected the Paynes' marriage, a close and loving one. In 1937, on the fortieth anniversary of their wedding, Dr. Payne wrote Miss Sue a long and touching and intimate love letter, so intimate it will not be reproduced here.

By the final year of his life, Dr. Payne was a tired man. The famous writers he had helped had mostly forgotten him or were dead. He now heard only from Stark Young. A month before his own death, Dr. Payne wrote his last letter to Robert Frost.

Home, 2104 Pearl Street
May 4, 1945

My dear "Robert Frost:"

You will perhaps be surprised to get a note from your old friend and admirer down here in Texas. I doubt if you have heard of a serious heart-attack which I suffered about three years ago. I had to lie flat on my back in bed for about six weeks, but I gradually got back on my job by going slow and taking care of myself under my good wife's supervision. When I reached the age of seventy about two years ago, the University put me on what we call "the half-time, half-pay" schedule. I lecture only three days in the week, and have only small classes now.

What I wish most to do at this time is to send you a word of greeting and offer my congratulations on your publication of a new type of verse for you in your poem called "A Masque of Reason." I made myself the proud possessor of a copy as soon as I saw the book in our University Book Store here. I promptly read the poem twice through—and I should like very much to have a copy of the limited-signed edition for my Frost collection. It is my intention to arrange to have my best books, including many first editions and signed copies, consigned to the University of Texas Rare Books Collection. You may recall the famous Wrenn Collection which is the basis of our rare book collection at the top of our very tall tower in our main building.

Mrs. Payne joins me in sending our sincere good wishes for your health and continued happiness. You will remember that Mrs. Payne and Mrs. Frost exchanged a number of letters in the earlier days, and I have some half dozen letters from you myself. So we are very proud of our Frost books and letters; and many of our friends have enjoyed looking over our collection of your first editions.

I wish you could come to the South again, but not in these treacherous war-time days. May your last days be days of peace and quiet and comfort is our wish.

Very sincerely, your admirer,
L. W. PAYNE, JR.

On June 17, 1945 Leonidas Warren Payne, Jr. suffered a second and fatal heart attack. He was seventy-one.

CHAPTER THIRTEEN

A Literary Legacy

DR. Payne inspired two generations with his patient teaching with a loving understanding of literature. His inspiring teaching and anthologies taught school children across America for decades. That is only part of his legacy. Dr. Payne's role as a critic completes the other part of his legacy.

Born at the end of the third quarter of the nineteenth century, L. W. Payne's life acted as a bridge between the Victorian era and the modern radicalism of twentieth century literature. Although he studied the radical literature and tried to understand it, he was never wholly convinced by it. He once complained that he had "been gorged on modern realism and on the stylistic monstrosities of the imitators of James Joyce."

The best summary of Professor Payne's feelings and opinions on the transition to twentieth century modern literature was given by him in a speech to the Lyceum Club of Dallas on January 9, 1941.

"When we come to the end of the nineteenth century and begin to listen to the later changes in style and method in the so-called *new verse*, our older ears already accustomed to the classic masterpieces of the past began to shake our heads and say "This will never do." Here come the reformers like Amy Lowell and Ezra Pound and invent the so-called Imagist Poetry. And the new free verse seemed so much like what one of my students called it, the "broken-toothed comb type of verse" that we older readers squinted our eyes at the experimenters and went our way to enjoy Tennyson or Bryant or Longfellow—the poets we were brought up on. However, there is one thing we older readers must keep always in mind, namely, that in literature and the other fine arts, just as in politics and philosophy new ideas come into being with each new generation or each new age.

I propose—as old as I am and as young and callow as much of the new poetry seems to me to be—to keep an open ear and a receptive mind, for what is good in the new types of literature as well as to retain my respect and my ultimate preference for the older types on which I cut my artistic teeth, as it were, and of which my own contemporaries were the creators and the propagators, the readers, and memorizers, and reciters from time to time.

Between 1913 and 1916 may be called the birth-time of the new American poetry. These new poets determined that whatever else they might be they would not be imitative. They were determined to eschew all trite words, phrases, cliches or out-worn figures of speech. Finally these new poets banished all sentimentality and slushy emotionalism, all saccharine twaddle and Puritanic moralizing in verse.

Personally I do not approve of the method of the younger poets and critics in attacking the older poets in order to find an audience for themselves.

The spoken word has become the written word. In an effort to avoid the commonplace the nineteenth century poet resorted to the abstract, forgetting that of things as common as cobblestones true poetry is made. The writer of today is in a struggle to the concrete.

The modern poet tries conscientiously to lop off every excrescence, every over-luxuriance, every needless decorative effect, and to leave only the hard, firm growth. Firmness and strength, realism and truth are his ideals. In fact, I think there is a little too much hardness and firmness, and hence too little grace and tenderness in modern poetry as a whole. Too much of the truth, in my judgment, becomes merely vulgar and inartistic. Too much precision and too great economy becomes unintelligible. Many over-enthusiastic disciples of repression have followed the difficult path of condensation, until they have nearly ended in obliteration, and have reduced their product to a sort of aesthetic shorthand intelligible to nobody but the author and his coterie.

For my part I always welcome radical experimentation in the arts. I am sure that artistic revolutions never lead backward. I am sure that out of every radical effort at reform some advance eventually comes, not always in the direction indicated by the experimenters, but surely in some direction. I think the free-versifiers have done a good turn to modern poetic style in limbering it up and giving it wider range and flexibility. I think the imagists have

140

added a great deal in the way of freshness and vivacity and modernity to our more recent poetry. If for no other reason we ought to be grateful to the new poets for their banishment of cliches, frozen poetical diction, classical allusions, antique archaisms, and all the older conventions. I realize that we must allow the new generations their own methods of artistic expression, or else we shall become static rather than progressive in art. I admit that I am a little old-fashioned myself, that I prefer to go along with the older poets for the most part, but I also admit that occasionally I get a thrill from some of the newer poetry. My chief objections have already been stated, namely I resent the unnecessary condensation and obscurity therefrom resulting, the false economy of language which makes for scrappiness instead of full aesthetic expression, and the forced effort to be clever and new which is constantly pushing the modern poets into extravagances and conceits which are entirely, in my judgment inartistic. Finally, if I should make out an indictment against the modern poets in one plea, it would be this: the new poets pay too much attention to trivialities and too little to the great underlying principles of life and art. Rarely does a modern poet touch one deeply. Rarely is one's soul stirred by the heroic, by the pathetic, by the sublime. The reader of modern poetry is no longer swept off his feet and uplifted as he was in the older days when he yielded to the grander sweep and the deeper tones of Milton, and Wordsworth, and Tennyson, and Browning, and Whitman. The modern poets deal too frequently in subtleties, in crotchets, in trivialities of life, too little in the verities, the deep mysteries, the great moral principles out of which great art is made."

Notes

CHAPTER ONE NOTES

[1] Robert Adger Law, "Leonidas Warren Payne, Jr. 1873–1945." *Studies in English.* (Austin: The University of Texas Press, 1945–46), 7–14. Permission to quote the remarks of Robert Adger Law was granted by Professor Law's son, Mr. Thomas H. Law, Fort Worth, Texas.

[2] Ibid.

[3] Edgar Lee Masters letter to L. W. Payne, Jr. October 20, 1919. Humanities Research Center. The University of Texas, Austin.

[4] Edgar Lee Masters letter to L. W. Payne, Jr. October 27, 1919. Humanities Research Center. The University of Texas, Austin.

[5] Lon Tinkle, *An American Original, The Life of J. Frank Dobie.* (Boston: Little, Brown and Company, 1978), 115.

[6] Stark Young letter to Mrs. L. W. Payne, Jr. June 26, 1945. Personal property of Sarah Payne Foxworth, Dallas, Texas.

[7] John Pilkington, ed. *Stark Young, A life in the Arts,* Letters, 1900–1962. (Baton Rouge: LSU Press, 1975), 1–2: 24.

[8] Ibid., 545.

[9] Ibid., 554.

CHAPTER TWO NOTES

Dr. Payne's daughter, Sarah Payne Foxworth, provided much of the manuscript material used for this chapter. The boxes of materials had been stored for many years at her home. These materials she uncovered for the author. Some of the Payne family history first appeared in a genealogy book Mrs. Foxworth published about her family. Mike Farmer researched Mrs. Foxworth's family history and information for this book was taken from that history.

CHAPTER THREE NOTES

[1] Lon Tinkle, *An American Original, The Life of J. Frank Dobie.* (Boston: Little, Brown and Company, 1978), 103.

[2] James T. Bratcher, *Analytical Index of The Texas Folklore Society.* (Dallas: SMU Press, 1973), 1–36: XV.

[3] Gay Wilson Allen, *Carl Sandburg.* (Minneapolis: University of Minnesota Press, 1972), 11–12.

CHAPTER FOUR NOTES

[1]Lon Tinkle, *American Original, The Life of J. Frank Dobie.* (Boston: Little, Brown and Company, 1978), 116.

[2]Ibid., 183.

[3]Ibid., 106.

[4]Ibid., 115.

J. Frank Dobie's dramatic letters to Dr. Payne were not discovered until 1982. Payne's daughter, Mrs. Sarah Payne Foxworth, found them packed away in a box in her home in Dallas. At the time of the author's research and writing, the Dobie letters were Mrs. Foxworth's personal property and she shared them generously with the author.

Dr. Payne's letters to Dobie are catalogued in The Humanities Research Center, The University of Texas, Austin.

CHAPTER FIVE NOTES

[1]Norman Friedman, *ee cummings, The Growth of a Writer.* (Carbondale, Illinois: Southern Illinois University Press, 1964), 26.

[2]S. V. Baum, ed. *E. E. Cummings and the Critics.* (East Lansing, Michigan: Michigan State University Press, 1962), vii.

[3]Charles Norman, *E. E. Cummings, The Magic-Maker.* (Boston: Little, Brown and Company, 1972), xii.

[4]Robert E. Wegner, *The Poetry and Prose of E. E. Cummings.* (New York: Harcourt, Brace and World, Inc., 1965), 44.

[5]Friedman, *Growth of a Writer,* 17.

[6]Norman, *Magic-Maker,* 236.

[7]Ibid., 239.

[8]Ibid., 246.

CHAPTER SIX NOTES

[1]Emery Neff, *Edwin Arlington Robinson.* (William Sloane Associates, 1948), 67.

[2]Herman Hagedorn, *Edwin Arlington Robinson, A Biography,* (New York: The Macmillan Company, Inc., 1938), 301.

[3]Ibid., 11–13.

[4]Neff, *Robinson,* 131–142.

[5]Ibid., 227–228.

[6]Hagedorn, *Robinson,* 362.

[7] Ibid., 367.

[8] Ibid., 373–374.

[9] Neff, *Robinson*, 209.

Edwin Arlington Robinson's statements about his art and its influences are contained in his letters to L. W. Payne, Jr., located in The Humanities Research Center, University of Texas, Austin.

CHAPTER EIGHT NOTES

[1] Lawrance Thompson, *Selected Letters of Robert Frost.* (New York: Holt Rinehart and Winston, 1964), 305, 344, 370.

[2] Ibid., 370.

[3] Elaine Barry, *Robert Frost on Writing.* (New Brunswick, New Jersey: Rutgers University Press, 1973), 105.

[4] Donald Hall, "Robert Frost Corrupted," *Atlantic Monthly*, March, 1982, 63.

Some of the information about Frost's visits to Texas was found in the letters of Mrs. Elinor Frost to Mrs. Payne, which are located in the Humanities Research Center, The University of Texas, Austin.

CHAPTER NINE NOTES

The information about Professor Payne's 1938 visit to England was put together from his personal notes on the trip which, at the time of my research, were uncatalogued material in the Humanities Research Center, University of Texas, Austin.

CHAPTER TEN NOTES

[1] Amy Lowell letter to L. W. Payne, Jr. September 19, 1919. Humanities Research Center, University of Texas, Austin.

[2] Harriet Monroe letter to L. W. Payne, Jr. April 19, 1919. Humanities Research Center, The University of Texas, Austin.

[3] W. B. Yeats letter to L. W. Payne, Jr. August 23, 1922. Humanities Research Center, The University of Texas, Austin.

[4] T. S. Eliot letter to L. W. Payne, Jr. November 7, 1927. Humanities Research Center, The University of Texas, Austin.

[5] Edwin Arlington Robinson letter to L. W. Payne, Jr. December 21, 1926. Humanities Research Center, The University of Texas, Austin.

[6] Charles Norman, *E. E. Cummings, The Magic-Maker.* (Boston: Little, Brown and Company, 1972), 184.

CHAPTER ELEVEN NOTES

[1] *Howard Mumford Jones, An Autobiography.* (Madison: The University of Wisconsin Press, 1979), 83–84.

[2] McKeithan's account, which he described to me in an interview, is almost exactly the account of Callaway he wrote in his unpublished memoirs.

[3] Robert A. Law, "Leonidas Warren Payne, Jr. 1873–1945." *Studies in English.* (Austin: The University of Texas Press, 1945–46), 7–14.

[4] Ibid.

[5] The remarks of Joseph M. Ray were taken from his unpublished memoirs and letters to the author.

CHAPTER TWELVE NOTES

[1] William A. Owens, *Three Friends: Bedichek, Dobie, Webb.* (Garden City, New York: Doubleday & Company, 1969), 252.

[2] Payne letter to Eugene Barker, November 22, 1941. Payne Papers, Ar-81-111, Barker History Center. The University of Texas, Austin.

[3] Eugene Barker Papers: General Correspondence, Box 2B100, Barker History Center. The University of Texas, Austin.

[4] Speeches of Eugene Barker. The Rainey Controversy, Eugene Barker Papers, The Barker History Center. The University of Texas, Austin.

[5] Burke Baker letter to Eugene Barker, November 21, 1923. Eugene Barker Papers: General Correspondence, November-December 1923, Barker History Center. The University of Texas, Austin.

[6] *Austin Daily Dispatch,* December 10, 1933.

A LIMITED EDITION OF 500 COPIES
WAS DESIGNED AND PRINTED BY DAVID HOLMAN
AT THE WIND RIVER PRESS, AUSTIN